The Piper's Pocket Guide to Embellishments

Light Embellishments

by Leonard Brewer Jr

Copyright © 2022 by Leonard Brewer Jr
All rights reserved.
ISBN: 979-8-9867478-0-4

I would like to thank my family for always being there. I would also like to thank my Pipe Major and the Midland Highlanders for giving me the gift of piping, which made this book possible. Huzzah!

Table of Contents

Embellishments 3
   Gracenotes 5
      G gracenote 5
      D gracenote 14
      E gracenote 18
   Thumb Gracenote 23
   Throws 25
      Light Throw on D (or Light D Throw) 25
      Heavy Throw on D (or Heavy D Throw) 27
      Half Throw on D (or Half D Throw) 30
      Half Heavy Throw on D (or Half Heavy D Throw) 30
   Single Strikes 31
      Low G Strike 31
      Strike to Low A 34
      Strike to B 34
      Strike to C 34
      Strike to E 35
      Strike to F 35
      Strike to High G (or Thumb Strike) 35
   Strikes 36
      G Strike to Low A 36
      G Strike to B 37
      G Strike to C 39
      G Strike to D 40
      G Strike to D with a C 42

    G Strike to E 43

    G Strike to F 45

Thumb Strikes 47

    Thumb Strike to Low A 47

    Thumb Strike to B 49

    Thumb Strike to C 51

    Thumb Strike to D 53

    Thumb Strike to D with a C 55

    Thumb Strike to E 57

    Thumb Strike to F 59

    Thumb Strike to High G 61

Half Strikes 63

    Half Strike to Low A 63

    Half Strike to B 63

    Half Strike to C 63

    Half Strike to D 64

    Half Strike to D with a C 64

    Half Strike to E 64

    Half Strike to F 65

    Half Strike to High G 65

Doublings 66

    Low G Doubling 66

    Low A Doubling 67

    B Doubling 69

    C Doubling 70

    D Doubling 72

    E Doubling 73

F Doubling 75

High G Doubling 76

High A Doubling 78

Thumb Doublings 80

Low G Thumb Doubling 80

Low A Thumb Doubling 81

B Thumb Doubling 83

C Thumb Doubling 85

D Thumb Doubling 87

E Thumb Doubling 88

F Thumb Doubling 90

Half Doublings 92

Low G Half Doubling 92

Low A Half Doubling 92

B Half Doubling 93

C Half Doubling 94

D Half Doubling 94

E Half Doubling 95

F Half Doubling 96

Grip or Leumluath 97

Grip 97

Half Grip 108

B Grip 109

G Grip 121

G Grip to Low A 121

G Grip to B 123

G Grip to C 124

  G Grip to D 126

  G Grip to D with a B 128

  G Grip to E 130

  G Grip to F 131

Thumb Grip 134

  Thumb Grip to Low A 134

  Thumb Grip to B 136

  Thumb Grip to C 138

  Thumb Grip to D 141

  Thumb Grip to D with a B 143

  Thumb Grip to E 145

  Thumb Grip to F 148

  Thumb Grip to High G 150

Half Grip 153

  Half Grip to Low A 153

  Half Grip to B 153

  Half Grip to C 154

  Half Grip to D 154

  Half Grip to D with a B 155

  Half Grip to E 156

  Half Grip to F 156

  Half Grip to High G 157

  Half Grip to High A 158

Tachum 161

Birls 163

  Birl 163

  A Birl 165

- G Birl 166
- Thumb Birl 168

Taorluaths 170
- Taorluath 170
- B Taorluath 175

Bublys 182
- Bubly 182
- Half Bubly 195

Pele (or Hub-A-Dub) 198
- Low A Pele 198
- B Pele 200
- C Pele 201
- D Pele 203
- D Pele with a C 205
- E Pele 207
- F Pele 208

Thumb Pele 211
- Thumb Pele's 211
- B Thumb Pele 213
- C Thumb Pele 216
- D Thumb Pele 218
- D Thumb Pele with a C 220
- E Thumb Pele 223
- F Thumb Pele 225
- High G Thumb Pele 227

Half Pele 230
- Half Pele 230

Double Strikes 234
Double Strikes 234
G Double Strikes 237
G Double Strikes to Low A 237
G Double Strike to B 238
G Double Strike on C 240
G Double Strike on D 241
G Double Strike on D with a C 243
G Double Strike on E 244
G Double Strike on F 246
Thumb Double Strikes 248
Thumb Double Strike on Low A 248
Thumb Double Strike on B 250
Thumb Double Strike on C 252
Thumb Double Strike on D 254
Thumb Double Strike on D with a C 256
Thumb Doubling Strike on E 258
Thumb Double Strike on F 260
Thumb Double Strike on High G 262
Half Double Strikes 264
Half Double Strike on Low A 264
Half Double Strike on B 266
Half Double Strike on C 268
Half Double Strike on D 270
Half Double Strike on D with a C 272
Half Double Strike on E 274
Half Double Strike on F 276

- Half Double Strike on High G 278
- Half Double Strike on High A 280

Triple Strike 282
- Triple Strikes 282

G Triple Strikes 285
- G Triple Strikes on Low A 285
- G Triple Strike on B 286
- G Triple Strike on C 288
- G Triple Strike on D 290
- G Triple Strike to D with a C 291
- G Triple Strike on E 293
- G Triple Strike on F 295

Thumb Triple Strikes 297
- Thumb Triple Strike on Low A 297
- Thumb Triple Strike on B 299
- Thumb Triple Strike on C 301
- Thumb Triple Strike on D 303
- Thumb Triple Strike on D with a C 305
- Thumb Triple Strike on E 307
- Thumb Triple Strike on F 309
- Thumb Triple Strike on High G 311

Half Triple Strikes 314
- Half Triple Strike on Low A 314
- Half Triple Strike on B 316
- Half Triple Strike on C 318
- Half Triple Strike on D 320
- Half Triple Strike on D with a C 322

> Half Triple Strike on E 324
>
> Half Triple Strike on F 326
>
> Half Triple Strike on High G 328
>
> Half Triple Strike on High A 330
>
> Double Gracenotes 332
>
>> D Double Gracenotes 332
>>
>> E Double Gracenotes 337
>>
>> F Double Gracenotes 347
>>
>> High G Double Gracenote 362
>>
>> High A Double Gracenote 387

Pictorial Index 422

> Low G 422
>
> Low A 423
>
> B 424
>
> C 425
>
> D 426
>
> E 427
>
> F 428
>
> High G 429
>
> High A 432

This Pocket Guide was designed to help pipers, both new and well-seasoned, have quick access to embellishments that are used in piping. It is not meant to teach you how to play the bagpipes, but to be a reference to help you learn the various embellishments and how to play them.

Each embellishment is shown, an explanation on how to play it is given, and then the embellishment is shown with what other notes it can be played with.

This book is written with the assumption that you know your bagpipe scale already. However, sometimes the 'note to finger' naming can get confusing, so a picture is provided to help you.

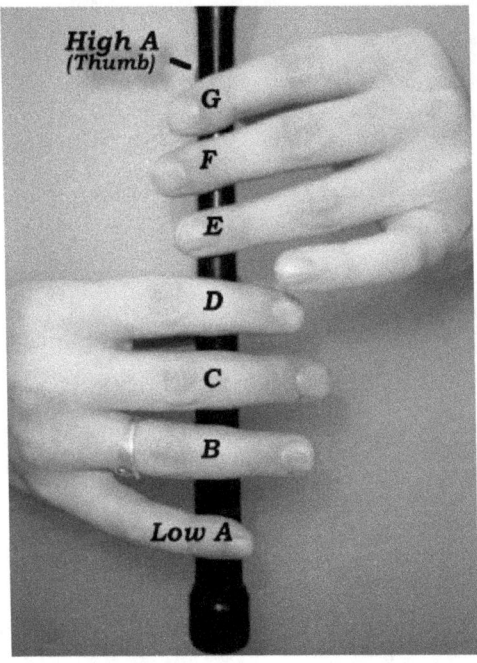

The finger is named for the hole that is *open* to make the sound. So, when you are playing a Low A, the Low A (right pinkie) finger is lifted off the hole.

Embellishments

Gracenotes

Gracenotes are quick finger movements that are played in between notes. A gracenote is played very fast and when played correctly has sort of a "pop" sound in between the notes.

G gracenote

Low G to Low G

1) Play Low G.
2) Lift up and then replace your G finger.

Low G to Low A

1) Play Low G.
2) Lift up your G gracenote and Low A finger at the same time.
3) Replace the G finger to form the Low A.

Low G to B

1) Play Low G.
2) Lift up your G gracenote, Low A and B fingers at the same time.
3) Replace the G finger to form the B.

Low G to C

1) Play Low G.
2) Lift up your G gracenote, B and C fingers at the same time.
3) Replace the G finger to form the C.

Low G to D

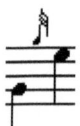
1) Play Low G.
2) Lift up your G gracenote, B, C and D fingers at the same time.
3) Replace the G finger to form the D.

Low G to E

1) Play Low G.
2) Lift up your G gracenote, Low A and E fingers at the same time.
3) Replace the G finger to form the E.

Low G to F

1) Play Low G.
2) Lift up your G gracenote, Low A, E and F fingers at the same time.
3) Replace the G finger to form the F.

Low A to Low G

1) Play Low A.
2) Lift up your G finger.
3) Replace the G gracenote and Low A finger at the same time to form a Low G.

Low A to Low A

1) Play Low A.
2) Lift up and then replace your G finger.

Low A to B

1) Play Low A.
2) Lift up your G gracenote and B finger at the same time.
3) Replace the G finger to form the B.

Low A to C

1) Play Low A.
2) Lift up your G gracenote, B and C fingers at the same time.
3) Replace the G gracenote and Low A fingers to form a C.

Low A to D

1) Play Low A.
2) Lift up your G gracenote, B, C and D fingers at the same time.
3) Replace the G gracenote and Low A finger to form a D.

Low A to E

1) Play Low A.
2) Lift up your G gracenote and E finger at the same time.
3) Replace the G finger to form an E.

Low A to F

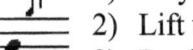
1) Play Low A.
2) Lift up your G gracenote, E and F fingers at the same time.
3) Replace the G finger to form an F.

B to Low G

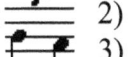
1) Play a B.
2) Lift up your G finger.
3) Replace the G gracenote, Low A, and B fingers at the same time to form a Low G.

B to Low A

1) Play a B.
2) Lift up your G finger.
3) Replace the G gracenote and B finger at the same time to form the Low A.

B to B

1) Play a B.
2) Lift up and then replace the G finger.

B to C

1) Play a B.
2) Lift up your G gracenote and C finger at the same time.
3) Replace the G gracenote and Low A finger at the same time to form the C.

B to D

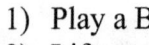

1) Play a B.
2) Lift up your G gracenote, C and D fingers at the same time.
3) Replace the G gracenote and Low A finger at the same time to form the D.

B to E

1) Play a B.
2) Lift up your G gracenote and E finger at the same time.
3) Replace the G gracenote and B finger at the same time to form an E.

B to F

1) Play a B.
2) Lift up your G gracenote, E and F fingers at the same time.
3) Replace the G gracenote and B fingers at the same time to form an F.

C to Low G

1) Play a C.
2) Lift up your G finger.
3) Replace the G gracenote, B and C fingers at the same time to form the Low G.

C to Low A

1) Play a C.
2) Lift up your G finger.
3) Replace the G gracenote, B and C fingers as well as raise the Low A finger at the same time to form a Low A.

C to B

1) Play a C.
2) Lift up your G finger.
3) Replace the G gracenote and B finger as well as raise the Low A finger at the same time to form a B.

C to C

1) Play a C.
2) Lift up and then replace the G finger.

C to D

1) Play a C.
2) Lift up your G gracenote and D finger at the same time.
3) Replace the G finger to form the D.

C to E

1) Play a C.
2) Lift up your G gracenote and E finger at the same time.
3) Replace the G gracenote, B and C fingers as well as raise the Low A finger at the same time to form an E.

C to F

1) Play a C.
2) Lift up your G gracenote, E and F fingers at the same time.
3) Replace the G gracenote, B and C fingers as well as raise the Low A finger at the same time to form an F.

D to Low G

1) Play a D.
2) Lift up your G finger.
3) Replace the G gracenote, D, C and B fingers at the same time to form a Low G.

D to Low A

1) Play a D.
2) Lift up your G finger.
3) Replace the G gracenote, D, C and B fingers as well as raise the Low A finger at the same time to form a Low A.

D to B

1) Play a D.
2) Lift up your G finger.
3) Replace the G gracenote, D and C finger as well as raise the Low A finger at the same time to form a B.

D to C

1) Play a D.
2) Lift up your G finger.
3) Replace the G gracenote and D finger at the same time to form a C.

D to D

1) Play a D.
2) Lift up and then replace the G finger.

D to E

1) Play a D.
2) Lift up your G gracenote and E finger at the same time.
3) Replace the G finger and reverse your lower hand at the same time to form an E.

D to F

1) Play a D.
2) Lift up your G gracenote, E and F fingers at the same time.
3) Replace the G finger and reverse your lower hand at the same time to form an F.

E to Low G

1) Play an E.
2) Lift up your G finger.
3) Replace the G gracenote, E and Low A fingers at the same time to form a Low G.

E to Low A

1) Play an E.
2) Lift up your G finger.
3) Replace the G gracenote and E finger at the same time to form a Low A.

E to B

1) Play an E.
2) Lift up your G finger.
3) Replace the G gracenote and E finger as well as raise the B finger at the same time to form a B.

E to C

1) Play an E.
2) Lift up your G finger.
3) Replace the G gracenote, E and Low A fingers as well as raise the B and C fingers at the same time to form a C.

E to D

1) Play an E.
2) Lift up your G finger.
3) Replace the G gracenote and E finger as well as reverse your lower hand all at the same time to form a D.

E to E

1) Play an E.
2) Lift up and then replace the G finger.

E to F

1) Play an E.
2) Lift up your G gracenote and F finger at the same time (both fingers on the left hand will be lifted).
3) Replace the G finger to form an F.

F to Low G

1) Play an F.
2) Lift up your G finger.
3) Replace your G gracenote, F, E, and Low A fingers at the same time to form a Low G.

F to Low A

1) Play an F.
2) Lift up your G finger.
3) Replace your G gracenote, F and E fingers at the same time to form a Low A.

F to B

1) Play an F.
2) Lift up your G finger.
3) Replace your G gracenote, F and E fingers as well as raise your B finger at the same time to form a B.

F to C

1) Play an F.
2) Lift up your G finger.
3) Replace your G gracenote, F, E and Low A fingers as well as raise your B and C fingers all at the same time to form a C.

F to D

1) Play an F.
2) Lift up your G finger.
3) Replace your G gracenote, F, E and reverse your lower hand all at the same time to form a D.

F to E

1) Play an F.
2) Lift up your G finger.
3) Replace your G gracenote and F finger at the same time to form an E.

F to F

1) Play an F.
2) Lift up and then replace the G finger.

The G gracenote can be played in between any note from Low G to F. You cannot play a G gracenote any higher than an F.

D gracenote

Low G to Low G

1) Play Low G.
2) Lift and then replace the D finger.

Low G to Low A

    1) Play Low G.
    2) Lift up your D gracenote and Low A finger at the same time.
    3) Replace the D finger to form a Low A.

Low G to B

    1) Play Low G.
    2) Lift up your D gracenote, Low A, and B fingers at the same time.
    3) Replace the D finger to form a B.

Low G to C*

    1) Play Low G.
    2) Lift up your D gracenote, Low A, B and C fingers (whole bottom hand) at the same time.
    3) Replace the D gracenote and Low A fingers at the same time to form a C.

*Or…If you have trouble performing the embellishment this way here is an alternative fingering that may help you.

    1) Play Low G.
    2) Lift up your D gracenote, B and C fingers at the same time.
    3) Replace the D finger to form a C.

Low A to Low G
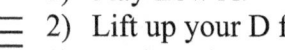

    1) Play Low A.
    2) Lift up your D finger.
    3) Replace the D gracenote and Low A finger at the same time to form a Low G.

Low A to Low A

    1) Play Low A.
    2) Lift and then replace the D finger.

Low A to B

1) Play Low A.
2) Lift up your D gracenote and B finger at the same time.
3) Replace the D finger to form the B.

Low A to C*

1) Play Low A.
2) Lift up your D gracenote, B and C fingers at the same time.
3) Replace the D gracenote and Low A finger at the same time to form a C.

*Or…If you have trouble performing the embellishment this way here is an alternative fingering that may help you.

3) First place the Low A finger onto the chanter followed by the D finger.

B to Low G

1) Play a B.
2) Lift up your D finger.
3) Replace your D gracenote, B and Low A fingers at the same time to form a Low G.

B to Low A

1) Play a B.
2) Lift up your D finger.
3) Replace your D gracenote and B finger at the same time to form a Low A.

B to B

1) Play a B.
2) Lift and then replace the D finger.

*B to C**

1) Play a B.
2) Lift up your D gracenote and C finger at the same time.
3) Replace your D gracenote and Low A finger at the same time to form a C.

*Or...If you have trouble performing the embellishment this way there is an alternative way that may help you.

3) First place your Low A finger on the chanter then place your D finger to form the C.

C to Low G

1) Play a C.
2) Lift up your D finger.
3) Replace your D gracenote, C and B fingers at the same time to form a Low G.

C to Low A

1) Play a C.
2) Lift up your D finger.
3) Replace your D gracenote, C and B fingers as well as lifting your Low A finger all at the same time to form a Low A.

C to B

1) Play a C.
2) Lift up your D finger.
3) Replace your D gracenote and C finger as well as lifting your Low finger all at the same time to form a B.

C to C

1) Play a C.
2) Lift and then replace the D finger.

The D gracenote can be played in between any note from Low G to C. You cannot play a D gracenote any higher than C.

E gracenote

Low G to Low G

1) Play a Low G.
2) Lift and then replace the E finger.

Low G to Low A

1) Play Low G.
2) Lift up your E gracenote and Low A finger at the same time.
3) Replace the E finger to form a Low A.

Low G to B

1) Play Low G.
2) Lift up your E gracenote, Low A, and B fingers at the same time.
3) Replace the E finger to form a B.

Low G to C

    1) Play Low G.
    2) Lift up your E gracenote, B and C fingers at the same time.
    3) Replace the E finger to form a C.

Low G to D

    1) Play Low G.
    2) Lift up your E gracenote, D, C and B fingers at the same time.
    3) Replace the E finger to form a D.

Low A to Low G

    1) Play Low A.
    2) Lift up your E gracenote finger.
    3) Replace the E gracenote and Low A finger at the same time to form a Low G.

Low A to Low A

    1) Play Low A.
    2) Lift and then replace the E finger.

Low A to B

    1) Play Low A.
    2) Lift up your E gracenote and B fingers at the same time.
    3) Replace the E finger to form a B.

Low A to C

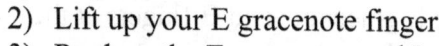

    1) Play Low A.
    2) Lift up your E, B and C fingers.
    3) Replace the E gracenote and Low A fingers at the same time to form a C.

Low A to D
1) Play Low A.
2) Lift up your E finger.
3) Replace the E finger and reverse the lower hand at the same time to form a D.

B to Low G
1) Play a B.
2) Lift up your E finger.
3) Replace the E gracenote, B and Low G fingers at the same time to form a Low G.

B to Low A
1) Play a B.
2) Lift up your E finger.
3) Replace the E gracenote and B fingers at the same time to form a Low A.

B to B
1) Play a B.
2) Lift and then replace the E finger.

B to C
1) Play a B.
2) Lift up your E gracenote and C finger at the same time.
3) Replace the E gracenote and Low A finger at the same time to form a C.

B to D
1) Play a B.
2) Lift up your E gracenote, C and D fingers at the same time.
3) Replace the E gracenote and Low A finger at the same time to form a D.

C to Low G

1) Play a C.
2) Lift up your E finger.
3) Replace the E gracenote, B and C fingers at the same time to form a Low G.

C to Low A

1) Play a C.
2) Lift up your E finger.
3) Replace the E gracenote, B and C fingers as well as raise the Low A finger all at the same time to form a Low A.

C to B

1) Play a C.
2) Lift up your E finger.
3) Replace the E gracenote and B finger as well as raise the Low A finger at the same time to form a B.

C to C

1) Play a C.
2) Lift up and then replace the E finger.

C to D

1) Play a C.
2) Lift up your E gracenote and D finger at the same time.
3) Replace the E finger to form a D.

D to Low G

1) Play a D.
2) Lift up your E gracenote finger.
3) Replace the E gracenote, D, B and C fingers at the same time to form a Low G.

21

D to Low A

1) Play a D.
2) Lift up your E finger.
3) Replace the E finger and reverse the lower hand at the same time to form a Low A.

D to B

1) Play a D.
2) Lift up your E finger.
3) Replace the E gracenote, D and C fingers as well as raise the Low A finger all at the same time to form a B.

D to C

1) Play a D.
2) Lift up your E finger.
3) Replace the E gracenote and D finger at the same time to form a C.

D to D

1) Play a D.
2) Lift and then replace the E finger.

The E gracenote can be played in between any note from Low G to D. You cannot play an E gracenote any higher than a D.

Thumb Gracenote

The thumb gracenote is played just like a normal gracenote only it requires that all of your fingers on your top hand be removed from the chanter for a brief moment.

Low G to High G

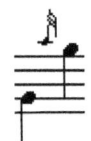

1) Play Low G.
2) Lift up your Low A finger and remove all of your top hand fingers including your thumb.
3) Place your High A finger back on the chanter forming a High G.

Low A to High G

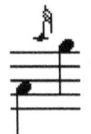

1) Play Low A.
2) Remove all of your top hand fingers including your thumb.
3) Place your High A finger back on the chanter forming a High G.

B to High G

1) Play a B.
2) Remove all of your top hand fingers including your thumb.
3) Place your High A and B finger back on the chanter forming a High G.

C to High G

1) Play a C.
2) Remove all of your top hand fingers including your thumb.
3) Place your High A, C, and B fingers back on the chanter as well as removing your Low A finger to form a High G.

D to High G

1) Play a D.
2) Remove all of your top hand fingers including your thumb.
3) Place your High A finger back on the chanter and reverse your lower hand at the same time forming a High G.

E to High G

1) Play an E.
2) Remove all of your top hand fingers including your thumb.
3) Place your High A finger back on the chanter forming a High G.

F to High G

1) Play an F.
2) Remove all of your top hand fingers including your thumb.
3) Place your High A finger back on the chanter forming a High G.

High G to High G

1) Play a High G.
2) Remove and then replace your High A finger.

The Thumb gracenote can be played in between any note from Low G to High G. You cannot play a thumb gracenote any higher than a High G.

Throws

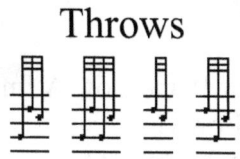

A throw is meant to be played evenly. Every note in the throw embellishment is to have an equal value, do not speed up or slow down portions of it, keep it all in the same timing. When played correctly it will have a ripple sound to it (except for the Heavy D Throw in which the first Low G is accented by holding it slightly longer than the rest of the notes.

Light Throw on D (or Light D Throw)
Note: The Light Throw on D and Heavy Throw on D are played differently but they are often used interchangeably. For instance, in a piece of music you may see a Light Throw on D but it is played like the Heavy Throw on D. The Light Throw on D is typically only used when playing Piobaireachd; the Heavy Throw on D is used in everything else.

Low G to Light Throw on D

1) Play Low G.
2) Do a D gracenote to C.
3) Play a D.

Low A to Throw on D

1) Play Low A.
2) Lower your Low A finger to form a Low G.
3) Do a D gracenote to C.
4) Play a D.

B to Light Throw on D

1) Play a B.
2) Lower your B and Low A fingers at the same time to form a Low G.
3) Do a D gracenote to C.
4) Play a D

C to Light Throw on D

1) Play a C.
2) Lower your C and B fingers at the same time to form a Low G.
3) Do a D gracenote to C.
4) Play a D.

D to Light Throw on D

1) Play a D.
2) Lower your D, C and B fingers at the same time to form a Low G.
3) Do a D gracenote to C.
4) Play a D.

E to Light Throw on D

1) Play an E.
2) Lower your E and Low A fingers at the same time to form a Low G.
3) Do a D gracenote to C.
4) Play a D.

F to Light Throw on D

1) Play an F.
2) Lower your F, E and Low A fingers at the same time to form a Low G.
3) Do a D gracenote to C.
4) Play a D.

High G to Light Throw on D

1) Play a High G.
2) Lower your G, F, E and Low A fingers at the same time to form a Low G.
3) Do a D gracenote to C.
4) Play a D.

High A to Light Throw on D

1) Play a High A.
2) Lower your High A, G, F, E and Low A fingers at the same time to form a Low G.
3) Do a D gracenote to C.
4) Play a D.

The Light Throw on D or Light D Throw can be played on any note but it always ends on a D.

Heavy Throw on D (or Heavy D Throw)

Low G to Heavy Throw on D

1) Play Low G.
2) Do a D gracenote while on Low G.
3) Play a C.
4) Play a D.

Low A to Heavy Throw on D
1) Play Low A.
2) Lower your Low A finger to form a Low G.
3) Do a D gracenote while on Low G.
4) Play a C.
5) Play a D.

B to Heavy Throw on D
1) Play a B.
2) Lower your B and Low A fingers at the same time to form a Low G.
3) Do a D gracenote while on Low G.
4) Play a C.
5) Play a D.

C to Heavy Throw on D
1) Play a C.
2) Lower your B and C fingers at the same time to form a Low G.
3) Do a D gracenote while on Low G.
4) Play a C.
5) Play a D.

D to Heavy Throw on D
1) Play a D.
2) Lower your D, C and B fingers at the same time to form a Low G.
3) Do a D gracenote while on Low G.
4) Play a C.
5) Play a D.

E to Heavy Throw on D
1) Play an E.
2) Lower your E and Low A finger to form a Low G.
3) Do a D gracenote while on Low G.
4) Play a C.
5) Play a D.

F to Heavy Throw on D

    1) Play an F.
    2) Lower your F, E and Low A fingers at the same time to form a Low G.
    3) Do a D gracenote while on Low G.
    4) Play a C.
    5) Play a D.

High G to Heavy Throw on D

    1) Play High G.
    2) Lower your G, F, E and Low A fingers at the same time to form a Low G.
    3) Do a D gracenote while on Low G.
    4) Play a C.
    5) Play a D.

High A to Heavy Throw on D

    1) Play High A.
    2) Lower your High A, G, F and Low A fingers at the same time to form a Low G.
    3) Do a D gracenote while on Low G.
    4) Play a C.
    5) Play a D.

The Heavy Throw on D or Heavy D Throw can be played on any note but it always ends on a D.

Half Throw on D (or Half D Throw)

Low G to Half Throw on D
1) Play Low G.
2) Do a D gracenote to C.
3) Play a D.

The Half Throw on D or Half D Throw can only be played from a Low G and it always ends on a D.

Half Heavy Throw on D (or Half Heavy D Throw)

Low G to Half Heavy Throw on D
1) Play Low G.
2) Do a D gracenote while still on Low G.
3) Play a C.
4) Play a D.

The Half Heavy Throw on D or Half Heavy D Throw can only be played from a Low G and it always ends on a D.

Single Strikes

Single strikes look just like a gracenote and they have the same note value, but instead of them appearing higher than the notes it is between they are lower than the notes.

Low G Strike

Low A – Low G Strike – Low A
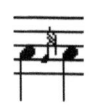
1) Play Low A.
2) Tap your Low A finger to sound a quick Low G and then lift it to play a Low A again.

Low A – Low G Strike – B

1) Play Low A.
2) Tap your Low A finger to sound a quick Low G and then lift your Low A and B fingers at the same time to form a B.

B – Low G Strike – Low A

1) Play a B.
2) Drop your B and Low A fingers to sound a quick Low G and then lift your Low A finger to form a Low A.

B – Low G Strike – B

1) Play a B.
2) Drop your B and Low A fingers to sound a quick Low G and then lift them both to form a B again.

B – Low G Strike – C

1) Play a B.
2) Drop your B and Low A fingers to sound a quick Low G and then lift your B and C fingers to form a C.

B – Low G Strike – D

1) Play a B.
2) Drop your B and Low A fingers to sound a quick Low G and then lift your B, C and D fingers to form a D.

C – Low G Strike – Low A

1) Play a C.
2) Drop your C and B fingers to sound a quick Low G and then lift your Low A finger to form a Low A.

C – Low G Strike – B

1) Play a C.
2) Drop your C and B fingers to sound a quick Low G and then lift your Low A and B fingers to form a B.

C – Low G Strike – C

1) Play a C.
2) Drop your C and B fingers to sound a quick Low G and then lift them both to form a C again.

C – Low G Strike – D

1) Play a C.
2) Drop your C and B fingers to sound a quick Low G and then lift your B, C and D fingers to form a D.

D – Low G Strike – Low A
1) Play a D.
2) Drop your D, C and B fingers to sound a quick Low G and then lift your Low A finger to form a Low A.

D – Low G Strike – B
1) Play a D.
2) Drop your D, C and B fingers to sound a quick Low G and then lift your Low A and B fingers to form a B.

D – Low G Strike – C
1) Play a D.
2) Drop your D, C and B fingers to sound a quick Low G and then lift your B and C fingers to form a C.

D – Low G Strike – D
1) Play a D.
2) Drop your D, C and B fingers to sound a quick Low G and then lift all three again to form a D.

The Strike to Low G can be played in between just about any note, but it cannot go any lower than a Low A.

Strike to Low A

B – Strike to Low A – B

1) Play a B.
2) Tap your B finger to sound a quick Low A and then lift it to form a B.

E – Strike to Low A – E

1) Play an E.
2) Tap your E finger to sound a quick Low A and then lift it to form a E.

Strike to B

C – Strike to B – C

1) Play a C.
2) Drop your C finger and raise your Low A finger to sound a quick B. Then raise your C finger and drop your Low A finger to form a C again.

Strike to C

D – Strike to C – D

1) Play a D.
2) Tap your D finger to sound a quick C and then raise it to form a D again.

Strike to E

F – Strike to E – F

1) Play an F.
2) Tap your F finger to sound a quick E and then raise it to form an F again.

Strike to F

High G – Strike to F – High G

1) Play High G.
2) Tap your G finger to sound a quick F and then raise it to form a High G again.

Strike to High G (or Thumb Strike)

High A – Strike to High G – High A

1) Play High A (rest your thumb above the High A hole).
2) Brush your thumb (High A finger) downward across the hole so that the chanter sounds a quick High G.

Strikes

G Strike to Low A

Low G – G Strike to Low A
1) Play Low G.
2) Do a G gracenote to Low A.
3) Tap your Low A finger to sound a quick Low G and then raise it to form a Low A again.

Low A – G Strike to Low A
1) Play Low A.
2) Do a G gracenote while still on Low A.
3) Tap your Low A finger to sound a quick Low G and then raise it to form a Low A again.

B – G Strike to Low A
1) Play a B.
2) Do a G gracenote to Low A.
3) Tap your Low A finger to sound a quick Low G and then raise it to form a Low A again.

C – G Strike to Low A
1) Play a C.
2) Do a G gracenote to Low A.
3) Tap your Low A finger to sound a quick Low G and then raise it to form a Low A again.

D – G Strike to Low A
1) Play a D.
2) Do a G gracenote to Low A.
3) Tap your Low A finger to sound a quick Low G and then raise it to form a Low A again.

E – G Strike to Low A

1) Play an E.
2) Do a G gracenote to Low A.
3) Tap your Low A finger to sound a quick Low G and then raise it to form a Low A again.

F – G Strike to Low A

1) Play an F.
2) Do a G gracenote to Low A.
3) Tap your Low A finger to sound a quick Low G and then raise it to form a Low A again.

The G Strike to Low A can be played in between any note from Low G to F and it always ends on a Low A. The G Strike to Low A cannot be played any higher than an F.

G Strike to B

Low G – G Strike to B

1) Play Low G.
2) Do a G gracenote to B.
3) Tap your Low A and B fingers to sound a quick Low G and then raise them to form a B again.

Low A – G Strike to B

1) Play Low A.
2) Do a G gracenote to B.
3) Tap your Low A and B fingers to sound a quick Low G and then raise them to form a B again.

B – G Strike to B

1) Play a B.
2) Do a G gracenote while still on B.
3) Tap your Low A and B fingers to sound a quick Low G and then raise them to form a B again.

C – G Strike to B

1) Play a C.
2) Do a G gracenote to B.
3) Tap your Low A and B fingers to sound a quick Low G and then raise them to form a B again.

D – G Strike to B

1) Play a D.
2) Do a G gracenote to B.
3) Tap your Low A and B fingers to sound a quick Low G and then raise them to form a B again.

E – G strike to B

1) Play an E.
2) Do a G gracenote to B.
3) Tap your Low A and B fingers to sound a quick Low G and then raise them to form a B again.

F – G Strike to B

1) Play an F.
2) Do a G gracenote to B.
3) Tap your Low A and B fingers to sound a quick Low G and then raise them to form a B again.

The G Strike to B can be played in between any note from Low G to F and it always ends on a B. The G Strike to B cannot be played any higher than an F.

G Strike to C

Low G – G Strike to C

1) Play Low G.
2) Do a G gracenote to C.
3) Tap your B and C fingers to sound a quick Low G and then raise them to form a C again.

Low A – G Strike to C

1) Play Low A.
2) Do a G gracenote to C.
3) Tap your B and C fingers to sound a quick Low G and then raise them to form a C again.

B – G Strike to C

1) Play a B.
2) Do a G gracenote to C.
3) Tap your B and C fingers to sound a quick Low G and then raise them to form a C again.

C – G Strike to C

1) Play a C.
2) Do a G gracenote while still on C.
3) Tap your B and C fingers to sound a quick Low G and then raise them to form a C again.

D – G Strike to C

1) Play a D.
2) Do a G gracenote to C.
3) Tap your B and C fingers to sound a quick Low G and then raise them to form a C again.

E – G Strike to C

1) Play an E.
2) Do a G gracenote to C.
3) Tap your B and C fingers to sound a quick Low G and then raise them to form a C again.

F – G Strike to C

1) Play an F.
2) Do a G gracenote to C.
3) Tap your B and C fingers to sound a quick Low G and then raise them to form a C again.

The G Strike to C can be played in between any note from Low G to F and it always ends on a C. The G Strike to C cannot be played any higher than an F.

G Strike to D

Low G – G Strike to D

1) Play Low G.
2) Do a G gracenote to D.
3) Tap your B, C and D fingers to sound a quick Low G and then raise them to form a D again.

Low A – G Strike to D

1) Play Low A.
2) Do a G gracenote to D.
3) Tap your B, C and D fingers to sound a quick Low G and then raise them to form a D again.

B – G Strike to D

1) Play a B.
2) Do a G gracenote to D.
3) Tap your B, C and D fingers to sound a quick Low G and then raise them to form a D again.

C – G Strike to D

1) Play a C.
2) Do a G gracenote to D.
3) Tap your B, C and D fingers to sound a quick Low G and then raise them to form a D again.

D – G Strike to D

1) Play a D.
2) Do a G gracenote while still on D.
3) Tap your B, C and D fingers to sound a quick Low G and then raise them to form a D again.

E – G Strike to D

1) Play an E.
2) Do a G gracenote to D.
3) Tap your B, C and D fingers to sound a quick Low G and then raise them to form a D again.

F – G Strike to D

1) Play an F.
2) Do a G gracenote to D.
3) Tap your B, C and D fingers to sound a quick Low G and then raise them to form a D again.

The G Strike to D can be played in between any note from Low G to F and it always ends on a D. The G Strike to D cannot be played any higher than an F.

G Strike to D with a C

Low G – G Strike to D with a C

1) Play Low G.
2) Do a G gracenote to D.
3) Tap your D finger to sound a quick C and then raise it to form a D again.

Low A – G Strike to D with a C

1) Play Low A.
2) Do a G gracenote to D.
3) Tap your D finger to sound a quick C and then raise it to form a D again.

B – G Strike to D with a C

1) Play a B.
2) Do a G gracenote to D.
3) Tap your D finger to sound a quick C and then raise it to form a D again.

C – G Strike to D with a C

1) Play a C.
2) Do a G gracenote to D.
3) Tap your D finger to sound a quick C and then raise it to form a D again.

D – G Strike to D with a C

1) Play a D.
2) Do a G gracenote while still on D.
3) Tap your D finger to sound a quick C and then raise it to form a D again.

E – G Strike to D with a C

1) Play an E.
2) Do a G gracenote to D.
3) Tap your D finger to sound a quick C and then raise it to form a D again.

F – G Strike to D with a C

1) Play an F.
2) Do a G gracenote to D.
3) Tap your D finger to sound a quick C and then raise it to form a D again.

The G Strike to D with a C can be played in between any note from Low G to F and it always ends on a D. The G Strike to D with a C cannot be played any higher than an F.

G Strike to E

Low G – G Strike to E

1) Play Low G.
2) Do a G gracenote to E.
3) Tap your E finger to sound a quick Low A and then raise it to form an E again.

Low A – G Strike to E

1) Play a Low A.
2) Do a G gracenote to E.
3) Tap your E finger to sound a quick Low A and then raise it to form an E again.

B – G Strike to E

1) Play a B.
2) Do a G gracenote to E.
3) Tap your E finger to sound a quick Low A and then raise it to form an E again.

C – G Strike to E

1) Play a C.
2) Do a G gracenote to E.
3) Tap your E finger to sound a quick Low A and then raise it to form an E again.

D – G Strike to E

1) Play a D.
2) Do a G gracenote to E.
3) Tap your E finger to sound a quick Low A and then raise it to form an E again.

E – G Strike to E

1) Play an E.
2) Do a G gracenote while still on E.
3) Tap your E finger to sound a quick Low A and then raise it to form an E again.

F – G Strike to E

1) Play an F.
2) Do a G gracenote to E.
3) Tap your E finger to sound a quick Low A and then raise it to form an E again.

The G Strike to E can be played in between any note from Low G to F and it always ends on an E. The G Strike to E cannot be played any higher than an F.

G Strike to F

Low G – G Strike to F

1) Play Low G.
2) Do a G gracenote to F.
3) Tap your F finger to sound a quick E and then raise it to form an F again.

Low A – G Strike to F

1) Play Low A.
2) Do a G gracenote to F.
3) Tap your F finger to sound a quick E and then raise it to form an F again.

B – G Strike to F

1) Play a B.
2) Do a G gracenote to F.
3) Tap your F finger to sound a quick E and then raise it to form an F again.

C – G Strike to F

1) Play a C.
2) Do a G gracenote to F.
3) Tap your F finger to sound a quick E and then raise it to form an F again.

D – G Strike to F

1) Play a D.
2) Do a G gracenote to F.
3) Tap your F finger to sound a quick E and then raise it to form an F again.

E – G Strike to F

1) Play an E.
2) Do a G gracenote to F.
3) Tap your F finger to sound a quick E and then raise it to form an F again.

F – G Strike to F

1) Play an F.
2) Do a G gracenote while still on F.
3) Tap your F finger to sound a quick E and then raise it to form an F again.

The G Strike to F can be played in between any note from Low G to F and it always ends on an F. The G Strike to F cannot be played any higher than an F.

Thumb Strikes

Thumb Strike to Low A

Low G – Thumb Strike to Low A

1) Play Low G.
2) Play a High A.
3) Play a Low A.
4) Tap your Low A finger to sound a quick Low G and then raise it to form a Low A again.

Low A – Thumb Strike to Low A

1) Play Low A.
2) Play a High A.
3) Play a Low A.
4) Tap your Low A finger to sound a quick Low G and then raise it to form a Low A again.

B – Thumb Strike to Low A

1) Play a B.
2) Play a High A.
3) Play a Low A.
4) Tap your Low A finger to sound a quick Low G and then raise it to form a Low A again.

C – Thumb Strike to Low A

1) Play a C.
2) Play a High A.
3) Play a Low A.
4) Tap your Low A finger to sound a quick Low G and then raise it to form a Low A again.

D – Thumb Strike to Low A
1) Play a D.
2) Play a High A.
3) Play a Low A.
4) Tap your Low A finger to sound a quick Low G and then raise it to form a Low A again.

E – Thumb Strike to Low A
1) Play an E.
2) Play a High A.
3) Play a Low A.
4) Tap your Low A finger to sound a quick Low G and then raise it to form a Low A again.

F – Thumb Strike to Low A
1) Play an F.
2) Play a High A.
3) Play a Low A.
4) Tap your Low A finger to sound a quick Low G and then raise it to form a Low A again.

High G – Thumb Strike to Low A
1) Play High G.
2) Play a High A.
3) Play a Low A.
4) Tap your Low A finger to sound a quick Low G and then raise it to form a Low A again.

The Thumb Strike to Low A can be played in between any note from Low G to High G and it always ends on a Low A. The Thumb Strike to Low A cannot be played any higher than High G.

Thumb Strike to B

Low G – Thumb Strike to B

1) Play Low G.
2) Play a High A.
3) Play a B.
4) Tap your Low A and B fingers to sound a quick Low G and then raise them to form a B again.

Low A – Thumb Strike to B

1) Play Low A.
2) Play a High A.
3) Play a B.
4) Tap your Low A and B fingers to sound a quick Low G and then raise them to form a B again.

B – Thumb Strike to B

1) Play a B.
2) Play a High A.
3) Play a B.
4) Tap your Low A and B fingers to sound a quick Low G and then raise them to form a B again.

C – Thumb Strike to B

1) Play a C.
2) Play a High A.
3) Play a B.
4) Tap your Low A and B fingers to sound a quick Low G and then raise them to form a B again.

D – Thumb Strike to B

1) Play a D.
2) Play a High A.
3) Play a B.
4) Tap your Low A and B fingers to sound a quick Low G and then raise them to form a B again.

E – Thumb Strike to B

1) Play an E.
2) Play a High A.
3) Play a B.
4) Tap your Low A and B fingers to sound a quick Low G and then raise them to form a B again.

F – Thumb Strike to B

1) Play an F.
2) Play a High A.
3) Play a B.
4) Tap your Low A and B fingers to sound a quick Low G and then raise them to form a B again.

High G – Thumb Strike to B

1) Play High G.
2) Play a High A.
3) Play a B.
4) Tap your Low A and B fingers to sound a quick Low G and then raise them to form a B again.

The Thumb Strike to B can be played in between any note from Low G to High G and it always ends on a B. The Thumb Strike to B cannot be played any higher than High G.

Thumb Strike to C

Low G – Thumb Strike to C

1) Play Low G.
2) Play a High A.
3) Play a C.
4) Tap your B and C fingers to sound a quick Low G and then raise them to form a C again.

Low A – Thumb Strike to C

1) Play Low A.
2) Play a High A.
3) Play a C.
4) Tap your B and C fingers to sound a quick Low G and then raise them to form a C again.

B – Thumb Strike to C

1) Play a B.
2) Play a High A.
3) Play a C.
4) Tap your B and C fingers to sound a quick Low G and then raise them to form a C again.

C – Thumb Strike to C

1) Play a C.
2) Play a High A.
3) Play a C.
4) Tap your B and C fingers to sound a quick Low G and then raise them to form a C again.

D – Thumb Strike to C

1) Play a D.
2) Play a High A.
3) Play a C.
4) Tap your B and C fingers to sound a quick Low G and then raise them to form a C again.

E – Thumb Strike to C

1) Play an E.
2) Play a High A.
3) Play a C.
4) Tap your B and C fingers to sound a quick Low G and then raise them to form a C again.

F – Thumb Strike to C

1) Play an F.
2) Play a High A.
3) Play a C.
4) Tap your B and C fingers to sound a quick Low G and then raise them to form a C again.

High G – Thumb Strike to C

1) Play High G.
2) Play a High A.
3) Play a C.
4) Tap your B and C fingers to sound a quick Low G and then raise them to form a C again.

The Thumb Strike to C can be played in between any note from Low G to High G and it always ends on a C. The Thumb Strike to C cannot be played any higher than High G.

Thumb Strike to D

Low G – Thumb Strike to D
1) Play Low G.
2) Play a High A.
3) Play a D.
4) Tap your B, C and D fingers to sound a quick Low G and then raise them to form a D again.

Low A – Thumb Strike to D
1) Play Low A.
2) Play a High A.
3) Play a D.
4) Tap your B, C and D fingers to sound a quick Low G and then raise them to form a D again.

B – Thumb Strike to D
1) Play a B.
2) Play a High A.
3) Play a D.
4) Tap your B, C and D fingers to sound a quick Low G and then raise them to form a D again.

C – Thumb Strike to D
1) Play a C.
2) Play a High A.
3) Play a D.
4) Tap your B, C and D fingers to sound a quick Low G and then raise them to form a D again.

D – Thumb Strike to D
1) Play a D.
2) Play a High A.
3) Play a D.
4) Tap your B, C and D fingers to sound a quick Low G and then raise them to form a D again.

E – Thumb Strike to D

1) Play an E.
2) Play a High A.
3) Play a D.
4) Tap your B, C and D fingers to sound a quick Low G and then raise them to form a D again.

F – Thumb Strike to D

1) Play an F.
2) Play a High A.
3) Play a D.
4) Tap your B, C and D fingers to sound a quick Low G and then raise them to form a D again.

High G – Thumb Strike to D

1) Play High G.
2) Play a High A.
3) Play a D.
4) Tap your B, C and D fingers to sound a quick Low G and then raise them to form a D again.

The Thumb Strike to D can be played in between any note from Low G to High G and it always ends on a D. The Thumb Strike to D cannot be played any higher than High G.

Thumb Strike to D with a C

Low G – Thumb Strike to D with a C
   1) Play Low G.
   2) Play a High A.
   3) Play a D.
   4) Tap your D finger to sound a quick C and then raise it to form a D again.

Low A – Thumb Strike to D with a C
   1) Play Low A.
   2) Play a High A.
   3) Play a D.
   4) Tap your D finger to sound a quick C and then raise it to form a D again.

B – Thumb Strike to D with a C
   1) Play a B.
   2) Play a High A.
   3) Play a D.
   4) Tap your D finger to sound a quick C and then raise it to form a D again.

C – Thumb Strike to D with a C
   1) Play a C.
   2) Play a High A.
   3) Play a D.
   4) Tap your D finger to sound a quick C and then raise it to form a D again.

D – Thumb Strike to D with a C
   1) Play a D.
   2) Play a High A.
   3) Play a D.
   4) Tap your D finger to sound a quick C and then raise it to form a D again.

E – Thumb Strike to D with a C
1) Play an E.
2) Play a High A.
3) Play a D.
4) Tap your D finger to sound a quick C and then raise it to form a D again.

F – Thumb Strike to D with a C
1) Play an F.
2) Play a High A.
3) Play a D.
4) Tap your D finger to sound a quick C and then raise it to form a D again.

High G – Thumb Strike to D with a C
1) Play High G.
2) Play a High A.
3) Play a D.
4) Tap your D finger to sound a quick C and then raise it to form a D again.

The Thumb Strike to D with a C can be played in between any note from Low G to High G and it always ends on a D. The Thumb Strike to D with a C cannot be played any higher than High G.

Thumb Strike to E

Low G – Thumb Strike to E

1) Play Low G.
2) Play a High A.
3) Play an E.
4) Tap your E finger to sound a quick Low A and then raise it to form an E again.

Low A – Thumb Strike to E

1) Play Low G.
2) Play a High A.
3) Play an E.
4) Tap your E finger to sound a quick Low A and then raise it to form an E again.

B – Thumb Strike to E

1) Play a B.
2) Play a High A.
3) Play an E.
4) Tap your E finger to sound a quick Low A and then raise it to form an E again.

C – Thumb Strike to E

1) Play a C.
2) Play a High A.
3) Play an E.
4) Tap your E finger to sound a quick Low A and then raise it to form an E again.

D – Thumb Strike to E

1) Play a D.
2) Play a High A.
3) Play an E.
4) Tap your E finger to sound a quick Low A and then raise it to form an E again.

E – Thumb Strike to E

1) Play an E.
2) Play a High A.
3) Play an E.
4) Tap your E finger to sound a quick Low A and then raise it to form an E again.

F – Thumb Strike to E

1) Play an F.
2) Play a High A.
3) Play an E.
4) Tap your E finger to sound a quick Low A and then raise it to form an E again.

High G – Thumb Strike to E

1) Play High G.
2) Play a High A.
3) Play an E.
4) Tap your E finger to sound a quick Low A and then raise it to form an E again.

The Thumb Strike to E can be played in between any note from Low G to High G and it always ends on an E. The Thumb Strike to E cannot be played any higher than High G.

Thumb Strike to F

Low G – Thumb Strike to F

1) Play Low G.
2) Play a High A.
3) Play an F.
4) Tap your F finger to sound a quick E and then raise it to form an E again.

Low A – Thumb Strike to F

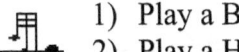
1) Play Low A.
2) Play a High A.
3) Play an F.
4) Tap your F finger to sound a quick E and then raise it to form an E again.

B – Thumb Strike to F

1) Play a B.
2) Play a High A.
3) Play an F.
4) Tap your F finger to sound a quick E and then raise it to form an E again.

C – Thumb Strike to F

1) Play a C.
2) Play a High A.
3) Play an F.
4) Tap your F finger to sound a quick E and then raise it to form an E again.

D – Thumb Strike to F

1) Play a D.
2) Play a High A.
3) Play an F.
4) Tap your F finger to sound a quick E and then raise it to form an E again.

E – Thumb Strike to F

1) Play an E.
2) Play a High A.
3) Play an F.
4) Tap your F finger to sound a quick E and then raise it to form an E again.

F – Thumb Strike to F

1) Play an F.
2) Play a High A.
3) Play an F.
4) Tap your F finger to sound a quick E and then raise it to form an E again.

High G – Thumb Strike to F

1) Play High G.
2) Play a High A.
3) Play an F.
4) Tap your F finger to sound a quick E and then raise it to form an E again.

The Thumb Strike to F can be played in between any note from Low G to High G and it always ends on an F. The Thumb Strike to F cannot be played any higher than High G.

Thumb Strike to High G

Low G – Thumb Strike to High G
1) Play Low G.
2) Play a High A.
3) Play a High G.
4) Tap your G finger to sound a quick F and then raise it to form a High G again.

Low A – Thumb Strike to High G

1) Play Low A.
2) Play a High A.
3) Play a High G.
4) Tap your G finger to sound a quick F and then raise it to form a High G again.

B – Thumb Strike to High G

1) Play a B.
2) Play a High A.
3) Play a High G.
4) Tap your G finger to sound a quick F and then raise it to form a High G again.

C – Thumb Strike to High G
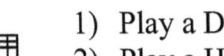
1) Play a C.
2) Play a High A.
3) Play a High G.
4) Tap your G finger to sound a quick F and then raise it to form a High G again.

D – Thumb Strike to High G
1) Play a D.
2) Play a High A.
3) Play a High G.
4) Tap your G finger to sound a quick F and then raise it to form a High G again.

E – Thumb Strike to High G

1) Play an E.
2) Play a High A.
3) Play a High G.
4) Tap your G finger to sound a quick F and then raise it to form a High G again.

F – Thumb Strike to High G

1) Play an F.
2) Play a High A.
3) Play a High G.
4) Tap your G finger to sound a quick F and then raise it to form a High G again.

High G – Thumb Strike to High G

1) Play High G.
2) Play a High A.
3) Play a High G.
4) Tap your G finger to sound a quick F and then raise it to form a High G again.

The Thumb Strike to High G can be played in between any note from Low G to High G and it always ends on a High G. The Thumb Strike to High G cannot be played any higher a High G.

Half Strikes

Half Strike to Low A

High A – Half Strike to Low A

1) Play High A.
2) Play a Low A.
3) Tap your Low A finger to sound a quick Low G and then raise it to form a Low A again.

Half Strike to B

High A – Half Strike to B

1) Play High A.
2) Play a B.
3) Tap your Low A and B fingers to sound a quick Low G and then raise them to form a B again.

Half Strike to C

High A – Half Strike to C

1) Play High A.
2) Play a C.
3) Tap your B and C fingers to sound a quick Low G and then raise it to form a C again.

Half Strike to D

High A – Half Strike to D
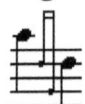
1) Play High A.
2) Play a D.
3) Tap your B, C and D fingers to sound a quick Low G and then raise them to form a D again.

Half Strike to D with a C

High A – Half Strike to D with a C

1) Play High A.
2) Play a D.
3) Tap your D finger to sound a quick C and then raise it to form a D again.

Half Strike to E

High A – Half Strike to E

1) Play High A.
2) Play an E.
3) Tap your E finger to sound a quick Low A and then raise it to form an E again.

Half Strike to F

High A – Half Strike to F

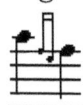
1) Play High A.
2) Play an F.
3) Tap your F finger to sound a quick E and then raise it to form an F again.

Half Strike to High G

High A – Half Strike to High G

1) Play High A.
2) Play a High G.
3) Tap your G finger to sound a quick F and then raise it to form a High G again.

Half Strikes are normally played from a High A.

Doublings

Low G Doubling

Low G to Low G Doubling

1) Play Low G.
2) Do a G gracenote followed by a D gracenote while still on Low G.

Low A to Low G Doubling

1) Play Low A.
2) Do a G gracenote to Low G.
3) Do a D gracenote while still on Low G.

B to Low G Doubling

1) Play a B.
2) Do a G gracenote to Low G.
3) Do a D gracenote while still on Low G.

C to Low G Doubling

1) Play a C.
2) Do a G gracenote to Low G.
3) Do a D gracenote while still on Low G.

D to Low G Doubling

1) Play a D.
2) Do a G gracenote to Low G.
3) Do a D gracenote while still on Low G.

E to Low G Doubling

1) Play an E.
2) Do a G gracenote to Low G.
3) Do a D gracenote while still on Low G.

F to Low G Doubling

1) Play an F.
2) Do a G gracenote to Low G.
3) Do a D gracenote while still on Low G.

The Low G Doubling can be played in between any note from Low G to F and it always ends on a Low G. The Low G Doubling cannot be played any higher than an F.

Low A Doubling

Low G to Low A Doubling

1) Play Low G.
2) Do a G gracenote to Low A.
3) Do a D gracenote while still on Low A.

Low A to Low A Doubling

1) Play Low A.
2) Do a G gracenote followed by a D gracenote while still on Low A.

B to Low A Doubling

1) Play a B.
2) Do a G gracenote to Low A.
3) Do a D gracenote while still on Low A.

C to Low A Doubling

1) Play a C.
2) Do a G gracenote to Low A.
3) Do a D gracenote while still on Low A.

D to Low A Doubling

1) Play a D.
2) Do a G gracenote to Low A.
3) Do a D gracenote while still on Low A.

E to Low A Doubling

1) Play an E.
2) Do a G gracenote to Low A.
3) Do a D gracenote while still on Low A.

F to Low A Doubling

1) Play an F.
2) Do a G gracenote to Low A.
3) Do a D gracenote while still on Low A.

The Low A Doubling can be played in between any note from Low G to F and it always ends on a Low A. The Low A Doubling cannot be played any higher than an F.

B Doubling

Low G to B Doubling

1) Play Low G.
2) Do a G gracenote to B.
3) Do a D gracenote while still on B.

Low A to B Doubling

1) Play Low A.
2) Do a G gracenote to B.
3) Do a D gracenote while still on B.

B to B Doubling

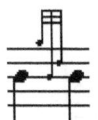
1) Play a B.
2) Do a G gracenote followed by a D gracenote while still on B.

C to B Doubling

1) Play a C.
2) Do a G gracenote to B.
3) Do a D gracenote while still on B.

D to B Doubling

1) Play a D.
2) Do a G gracenote to B.
3) Do a D gracenote while still on B.

E to B Doubling

1) Play an E.
2) Do a G gracenote to B.
3) Do a D gracenote while still on B.

F to B Doubling

1) Play an F.
2) Do a G gracenote to B.
3) Do a D gracenote while still on B.

The B Doubling can be played in between any note from Low G to F and it always ends on a B. The B Doubling cannot be played any higher than an F.

C Doubling

Low G to C Doubling

1) Play Low G.
2) Do a G gracenote to C.
3) Do a D gracenote while still on C.

Low A to C Doubling

1) Play Low A.
2) Do a G gracenote to C.
3) Do a D gracenote while still on C.

B to C Doubling

1) Play a B.
2) Do a G gracenote to C.
3) Do a D gracenote while still on C.

C to C Doubling

1) Play a C.
2) Do a G gracenote followed by a D gracenote while still on C.

D to C Doubling

1) Play a D.
2) Do a G gracenote to C.
3) Do a D gracenote while still on C.

E to C Doubling

1) Play an E.
2) Do a G gracenote to C.
3) Do a D gracenote while still on C.

F to C Doubling

1) Play an F.
2) Do a G gracenote to C.
3) Do a D gracenote while still on C.

The C Doubling can be played in between any note from Low G to F and it always ends on a C. The C Doubling cannot be played any higher than an F.

D Doubling

Low G to D Doubling
    1) Play Low G.
    2) Do a G gracenote to D.
    3) Do an E gracenote while still on D.

Low A to D Doubling
    1) Play Low A.
    2) Do a G gracenote to D.
    3) Do an E gracenote while still on D.

B to D Doubling
    1) Play a B.
    2) Do a G gracenote to D.
    3) Do an E gracenote while still on D.

C to D Doubling
    1) Play a C.
    2) Do a G gracenote to D.
    3) Do an E gracenote while still on D.

D to D Doubling

1) Play a D.
2) Do a G gracenote followed by an E gracenote while still on D.

E to D Doubling

1) Play an E.
2) Do a G gracenote to D.
3) Do an E gracenote while still on D.

F to D Doubling

1) Play an F.
2) Do a G gracenote to D.
3) Do an E gracenote while still on D.

The D Doubling can be played in between any note from Low G to F and it always ends on a D. The D Doubling cannot be played any higher than an F.

E Doubling

Low G to E Doubling

1) Play Low G.
2) Do a G gracenote to E.
3) Do an F gracenote by lifting and then replacing your F finger while still on E.

Low A to E Doubling

1) Play Low A.
2) Do a G gracenote to E.
3) Do an F gracenote by lifting and then replacing your F finger while still on E.

B to E Doubling

1) Play a B.
2) Do a G gracenote to E.
3) Do an F gracenote by lifting and then replacing your F finger while still on E.

C to E Doubling

1) Play a C.
2) Do a G gracenote to E.
3) Do an F gracenote by lifting and then replacing your F finger while still on E.

D to E Doubling

1) Play a D.
2) Do a G gracenote to E.
3) Do an F gracenote by lifting and then replacing your F finger while still on E.

E to E Doubling

1) Play an E.
2) Do a G gracenote while on E.
3) Do an F gracenote by lifting and then replacing your F finger while still on E.

F to E Doubling

1) Play an F.
2) Do a G gracenote to E.
3) Do an F gracenote by lifting and then replacing your F finger while still on E.

The E Doubling can be played in between any note from Low G to F and it always ends on an E. The E Doubling cannot be played any higher than an F.

F Doubling

Low G to F Doubling

1) Play Low G.
2) Do a G gracenote to F followed by another G gracenote while still on F.

Low A to F Doubling

1) Play Low A.
2) Do a G gracenote to F followed by another G gracenote while still on F.

B to F Doubling

1) Play a B.
2) Do a G gracenote to F followed by another G gracenote while still on F.

C to F Doubling

1) Play a C.
2) Do a G gracenote to F followed by another G gracenote while still on F.

D to F Doubling

1) Play a D.
2) Do a G gracenote to F followed by another G gracenote while still on F.

E to F Doubling

1) Play an E.
2) Do a G gracenote to F followed by another G gracenote while still on F.

F to F Doubling

1) Play an F.
2) Do two G gracenotes in a row on F.

The F Doubling can be played in between any note from Low G to F and it always ends on an F. The F Doubling cannot be played any higher than an F.

High G Doubling

Low G to High G Doubling

1) Play Low G.
2) Do a G gracenote to F.
3) Lift your G finger to form a High G.

Low A to High G Doubling

1) Play Low A.
2) Do a G gracenote to F.
3) Lift your G finger to form a High G.

B to High G Doubling

1) Play a B.
2) Do a G gracenote to F.
3) Lift your G finger to form a High G.

C to High G Doubling

1) Play a C.
2) Do a G gracenote to F.
3) Lift your G finger to form a High G.

D to High G Doubling

1) Play a D.
2) Do a G gracenote to F.
3) Lift your G finger to form a High G.

E to High G Doubling

1) Play an E.
2) Do a G gracenote to F.
3) Lift your G finger to form a High G.

F to High G Doubling

1) Play an F.
2) Do a G gracenote while on F and then lift your G finger to form a High G.

The High G Doubling can be played in between any note from Low G to F and it always ends on a High G. The High G Doubling cannot go any higher than an F.

High A Doubling

Low G to High A Doubling

1) Play Low G.
2) Play a High A and immediately brush your thumb across the hole sounding a quick High G.

Low A to High A Doubling

1) Play Low A.
2) Play a High A and immediately brush your thumb across the hole sounding a quick High G.

B to High A Doubling

1) Play a B.
2) Play a High A and immediately brush your thumb across the hole sounding a quick High G.

C to High A Doubling

1) Play a C.
2) Play a High A and immediately brush your thumb across the hole sounding a quick High G.

D to High A Doubling

   1) Play a D.
   2) Play a High A and immediately brush your thumb across the hole sounding a quick High G.

E to High A Doubling

   1) Play an E.
   2) Play a High A and immediately brush your thumb across the hole sounding a quick High G.

F to High A Doubling

   1) Play an F.
   2) Play a High A and immediately brush your thumb across the hole sounding a quick High G.

High G to High A Doubling
   1) Play High G.
   2) Play a High A and immediately brush your thumb across the hole sounding a quick High G.

The High A Doubling can be played in between any note from Low G to High G and it always ends on a High A. The High G Doubling cannot be played any higher than a High G. When the thumb is brushed across the hole it should start above the High A hole, go downward across the hole, and finish below the High A hole.

Thumb Doublings

Low G Thumb Doubling

Low G to Low G Thumb Doubling

1) Play Low G.
2) Play a High A
3) Play a Low G again.
4) Do a D gracenote while still on Low G.

Low A to Low G Thumb Doubling

1) Play Low A.
2) Play a High A.
3) Play a Low G.
4) Do a D gracenote while still on Low G.

B to Low G Thumb Doubling

1) Play a B.
2) Play a High A.
3) Play a Low G.
4) Do a D gracenote while still on Low G.

C to Low G Thumb Doubling

1) Play a C.
2) Play a High A.
3) Play a Low G.
4) Do a D gracenote while still on Low G.

D to Low G Thumb Doubling

1) Play a D.
2) Play a High A.
3) Play a Low G.
4) Do a D gracenote while still on Low G.

E to Low G Thumb Doubling

1) Play an E.
2) Play a High A.
3) Play a Low G.
4) Do a D gracenote while still on Low G.

F to Low G Thumb Doubling

1) Play an F.
2) Play a High A.
3) Play a Low G.
4) Do a D gracenote while still on Low G.

High G to Low G Thumb Doubling

1) Play High G.
2) Play a High A.
3) Play a Low G.
4) Do a D gracenote while still on Low G.

The Low G Thumb Doubling can be played in between any note from Low G to High G and it always ends on a Low G. The Low G Thumb Doubling cannot be played any higher than High G.

Low A Thumb Doubling

Low G to Low A Thumb Doubling

1) Play Low G.
2) Play a High A.
3) Play a Low A.
4) Do a D gracenote while still on Low A.

81

Low A to Low A Thumb Doubling

1) Play Low A.
2) Play a High A.
3) Play a Low A.
4) Do a D gracenote while still on Low A.

B to Low A Thumb Doubling

1) Play a B.
2) Play a High A.
3) Play a Low A.
4) Do a D gracenote while still on Low A.

C to Low A Thumb Doubling

1) Play a C.
2) Play a High A.
3) Play a Low A.
4) Do a D gracenote while still on Low A.

D to Low A Thumb Doubling

1) Play a D.
2) Play a High A.
3) Play a Low A.
4) Do a D gracenote while still on Low A.

E to Low A Thumb Doubling

1) Play an E.
2) Play a High A.
3) Play a Low A.
4) Do a D gracenote while still on Low A.

F to Low A Thumb Doubling

1) Play an F.
2) Play a High A.
3) Play a Low A.
4) Do a D gracenote while still on Low A.

High G to Low A Thumb Doubling

    1) Play High G.
    2) Play a High A.
    3) Play a Low A.
    4) Do a D gracenote while still on Low A.

The Low A Thumb Doubling can be played in between any note from Low G to High G and always ends on a Low A. The Low A Thumb Doubling cannot be played any higher than High G.

B Thumb Doubling

Low G to B Thumb Doubling

    1) Play Low G.
    2) Play a High A.
    3) Play a B.
    4) Do a D gracenote while still on B.

Low A to B Thumb Doubling

    1) Play Low A.
    2) Play a High A.
    3) Play a B.
    4) Do a D gracenote while still on B.

B to B Thumb Doubling

    1) Play a B.
    2) Play a High A.
    3) Play a B.
    4) Do a D gracenote while still on B.

C to B Thumb Doubling

1) Play a C.
2) Play a High A.
3) Play a B.
4) Do a D gracenote while still on B.

D to B Thumb Doubling

1) Play a D.
2) Play a High A.
3) Play a B.
4) Do a D gracenote while still on B.

E to B Thumb Doubling

1) Play an E.
2) Play a High A.
3) Play a B.
4) Do a D gracenote while still on B.

F to B Thumb Doubling

1) Play an F.
2) Play a High A.
3) Play a B.
4) Do a D gracenote while still on B.

High G to B Thumb Doubling

1) Play High G.
2) Play a High A.
3) Play a B.
4) Do a D gracenote while still on B.

The B Thumb Doubling can be played in between any note from Low G to High G and it always ends on a B. The B Thumb Doubling cannot be played any higher than High G.

C Thumb Doubling

Low G to C Thumb Doubling

1) Play Low G.
2) Play a High A.
3) Play a C.
4) Do a D gracenote while still on C.

Low A to C Thumb Doubling

1) Play Low A.
2) Play a High A.
3) Play a C.
4) Do a D gracenote while still on C.

B to C Thumb Doubling

1) Play a B.
2) Play a High A.
3) Play a C.
4) Do a D gracenote while still on C.

C to C Thumb Doubling

1) Play a C.
2) Play a High A.
3) Play a C.
4) Do a D gracenote while still on C.

D to C Thumb Doubling

1) Play a D.
2) Play a High A.
3) Play a C.
4) Do a D gracenote while still on C.

E to C Thumb Doubling

1) Play an E.
2) Play a High A.
3) Play a C.
4) Do a D gracenote while still on C.

F to C Thumb Doubling

1) Play an F.
2) Play a High A.
3) Play a C.
4) Do a D gracenote while still on C.

High G to C Thumb Doubling

1) Play High G.
2) Play a High A.
3) Play a C.
4) Do a D gracenote while still on C.

The C Thumb Doubling can be played in between any note from Low G to High G and it always ends on a C. The C Thumb Doubling cannot be played any higher than High G.

D Thumb Doubling

Low G to D Thumb Doubling

1) Play Low G.
2) Play a High A.
3) Play a D.
4) Do an E gracenote while still on D.

Low A to D Thumb Doubling

1) Play Low A.
2) Play a High A.
3) Play a D.
4) Do an E gracenote while still on D.

B to D Thumb Doubling

1) Play a B.
2) Play a High A.
3) Play a D.
4) Do an E gracenote while still on D.

C to D Thumb Doubling

1) Play a C.
2) Play a High A.
3) Play a D.
4) Do an E gracenote while still on D.

D to D Thumb Doubling

1) Play a D.
2) Play a High A.
3) Play a D.
4) Do an E gracenote while still on D.

E to D Thumb Doubling

1) Play an E.
2) Play a High A.
3) Play a D.
4) Do an E gracenote while still on D.

F to D Thumb Doubling

1) Play an F.
2) Play a High A.
3) Play a D.
4) Do an E gracenote while still on D.

High G to D Thumb Doubling

1) Play High G.
2) Play a High A.
3) Play a D.
4) Do an E gracenote while still on D.

The D Thumb Doubling can be played in between any note from Low G to High G and it always ends on a D. The D Thumb Doubling cannot be played any higher than High G.

E Thumb Doubling

Low G to E Thumb Doubling

1) Play Low G.
2) Play a High A.
3) Play an E.
4) Do an F gracenote while still on E.

Low A to E Thumb Doubling

1) Play Low A.
2) Play a High A.
3) Play an E.
4) Do an F gracenote while still on E.

B to E Thumb Doubling

1) Play a B.
2) Play a High A.
3) Play an E.
4) Do an F gracenote while still on E.

C to E Thumb Doubling

1) Play a C.
2) Play a High A.
3) Play an E.
4) Do an F gracenote while still on E.

D to E Thumb Doubling

1) Play a D.
2) Play a High A.
3) Play an E.
4) Do an F gracenote while still on E.

E to E Thumb Doubling

1) Play an E.
2) Play a High A.
3) Play an E.
4) Do an F gracenote while still on E.

F to E Thumb Doubling

1) Play an F.
2) Play a High A.
3) Play an E.
4) Do an F gracenote while still on E.

High G to E Thumb Doubling

1) Play High G.
2) Play a High A.
3) Play an E.
4) Do an F gracenote while still on E.

The E Thumb Doubling can be played in between any note from Low G to High G and always ends on an E. The E Thumb Doubling cannot be played any higher than High G.

F Thumb Doubling

Low G to F Thumb Doubling

1) Play Low G.
2) Play a High A.
3) Play an F.
4) Do a G gracenote while still on F.

Low A to F Thumb Doubling

1) Play Low A.
2) Play a High A.
3) Play an F.
4) Do a G gracenote while still on F.

B to F Thumb Doubling

1) Play a B.
2) Play a High A.
3) Play an F.
4) Do a G gracenote while still on F.

C to F Thumb Doubling

1) Play a B.
2) Play a High A.
3) Play an F.
4) Do a G gracenote while still on F.

D to F Thumb Doubling

1) Play a D.
2) Play a High A.
3) Play an F.
4) Do a G gracenote while still on F.

E to F Thumb Doubling

1) Play an E.
2) Play a High A.
3) Play an F.
4) Do a G gracenote while still on F.

F to F Thumb Doubling

1) Play an F.
2) Play a High A.
3) Play an F.
4) Do a G gracenote while still on F.

High G to F Thumb Doubling

1) Play High G.
2) Play a High A.
3) Play an F.
4) Do a G gracenote while still on F.

The F Thumb Doubling can be played in between any note from Low G to High G and it always ends on an F. The F Thumb Doubling cannot be played any higher than High G.

Half Doublings

Low G Half Doubling

High G to Low G Half Doubling
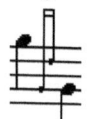
1) Play High G.
2) Play a Low G.
3) Do a D gracenote while still on Low G.

High A to Low G Half Doubling

1) Play a High A.
2) Play a Low G.
3) Do a D gracenote while still on Low G.

The Low G Half Doubling can only be played on High G and High A and it always ends on a Low G.

Low A Half Doubling

High G to Low A Half Doubling

1) Play High G.
2) Play a Low A.
3) Do a D gracenote while still on Low A.

High A to Low A Half Doubling

   1) Play High A.
   2) Play a Low A.
   3) Do a D gracenote while still on Low A.

The Low A Half Doubling can only be played on High G and High A and it always ends on a Low A.

B Half Doubling

High G to B Half Doubling

   1) Play High G.
   2) Play a B.
   3) Do a D gracenote while still on B.

High A to B Half Doubling

   1) Play a High A.
   2) Play a B.
   3) Do a D gracenote while still on B.

The B Half Doubling can only be played on High G and High A and it always ends on a B.

C Half Doubling

High G to C Half Doubling
1) Play High G.
2) Play a C.
3) Do a D gracenote while still on C.

High A to C Half Doubling
1) Play a High A.
2) Play a C.
3) Do a D gracenote while still on C.

The C Half Doubling can only be played on High G and High A and it always ends on a C.

D Half Doubling

High G to D Half Doubling
1) Play High G.
2) Play a D.
3) Do an E gracenote while still on D.

High A to D Half Doubling

 1) Play High A.
 2) Play a D.
 3) Do an E gracenote while still on D.

The D Half Doubling can only be played on High G and High A and it always ends on a D.

E Half Doubling

High G to E Half Doubling

 1) Play High G.
 2) Play an E.
 3) Do an F gracenote while still on E.

High A to E Half Doubling

 1) Play High A.
 2) Play an E.
 3) Do an F gracenote while still on E.

The E Half Doubling can only be played from High G and High A and it always ends on an E.

F Half Doubling

High G to F Half Doubling

    1) Play High G.
    2) Play an F.
    3) Do a G gracenote while still on F.

High A to F Half Doubling
    1) Play High A.
    2) Play an F.
    3) Do a G gracenote while still on F.

The F Half Doubling can only be play on High G and High A and it always ends on an F.

Grip or Leumluath

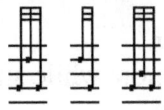

Grip

Low A – Grip – Low A

1) Play Low A.
2) Play a Low G.
3) Do a D gracenote while still on Low G.
4) Play a Low A.

Low A – Grip – B

1) Play Low A.
2) Play a Low G.
3) Do a D gracenote while still on Low G.
4) Play a B.

Low A – Grip – C

1) Play Low A.
2) Play a Low G.
3) Do a D gracenote while still on Low G.
4) Play a C.

Low A – Grip – D

1) Play Low A.
2) Play a Low G.
3) Do a D gracenote while still on Low G.
4) Play a D.

Low A – Grip – E

1) Play Low A.
2) Play a Low G.
3) Do a D gracenote while still on Low G.
4) Play an E.

Low A – Grip – F

1) Play Low A.
2) Play a Low G.
3) Do a D gracenote while still on Low G.
4) Play an F.

Low A – Grip – High G

1) Play Low A.
2) Play a Low G.
3) Do a D gracenote while still on Low G.
4) Play a High G.

Low A – Grip – High A

1) Play Low A.
2) Play a Low G.
3) Do a D gracenote while still on Low G.
4) Play a High A.

B – Grip – Low A

1) Play a B.
2) Play a Low G.
3) Do a D gracenote while still on Low G.
4) Play a Low A

B – Grip – B

1) Play a B.
2) Play a Low G.
3) Do a D gracenote while still on Low G.
4) Play a B.

B – Grip – C

1) Play a B.
2) Play a Low G.
3) Do a D gracenote while still on Low G.
4) Play a C.

B – Grip – D

1) Play a B.
2) Play a Low G.
3) Do a D gracenote while still on Low G.
4) Play a D.

B – Grip – E

1) Play a B.
2) Play a Low G.
3) Do a D gracenote while still on Low G.
4) Play an E.

B – Grip – F

1) Play a B.
2) Play a Low G.
3) Do a D gracenote while still on Low G.
4) Play an F.

B – Grip – High G

1) Play a B.
2) Play a Low G.
3) Do a D gracenote while still on Low G.
4) Play a High G.

B – Grip – High A

1) Play a B.
2) Play a Low G.
3) Do a D gracenote while still on Low G.
4) Play a High A.

C – Grip – Low A

1) Play a C.
2) Play a Low G.
3) Do a D gracenote while still on Low G.
4) Play a Low A.

C – Grip – B

1) Play a C.
2) Play a Low G.
3) Do a D gracenote while still on Low G.
4) Play a B.

C – Grip – C

1) Play a C.
2) Play a Low G.
3) Do a D gracenote while still on Low G.
4) Play a C.

C – Grip – D

1) Play a C.
2) Play a Low G.
3) Do a D gracenote while still on Low G.
4) Play a D.

C – Grip – E

1) Play a C.
2) Play a Low G.
3) Do a D gracenote while still on Low G.
4) Play an E.

C – Grip – F

1) Play a C.
2) Play a Low G.
3) Do a D gracenote while still on Low G.
4) Play an F.

C – Grip – High G

1) Play a C.
2) Play a Low G.
3) Do a D gracenote while still on Low G.
4) Play a High G.

C – Grip – High A

1) Play a C.
2) Play a Low G.
3) Do a D gracenote while still on Low G.
4) Play a High A.

D – Grip – Low A

1) Play a D.
2) Play a Low G.
3) Do a D gracenote while still on Low G.
4) Play a Low A.

D – Grip – B

1) Play a D.
2) Play a Low G.
3) Do a D gracenote while still on Low G.
4) Play a B.

D – Grip – C

1) Play a D.
2) Play a Low G.
3) Do a D gracenote while still on Low G.
4) Play a C.

D – Grip – D

1) Play a D.
2) Play a Low G.
3) Do a D gracenote while still on Low G.
4) Play a D.

D – Grip – E

1) Play a D.
2) Play a Low G.
3) Do a D gracenote while still on Low G.
4) Play an E.

D – Grip – F

1) Play a D.
2) Play a Low G.
3) Do a D gracenote while still on Low G.
4) Play an F.

D – Grip – High G

1) Play a D.
2) Play a Low G.
3) Do a D gracenote while still on Low G.
4) Play a High G.

D – Grip – High A

1) Play a D.
2) Play a Low G.
3) Do a D gracenote while still on Low G.
4) Play a High A.

E – Grip – Low A

1) Play an E.
2) Play a Low G.
3) Do a D gracenote while still on Low G.
4) Play a Low A.

E – Grip – B

1) Play an E.
2) Play a Low G.
3) Do a D gracenote while still on Low G.
4) Play a B.

E – Grip – C

1) Play an E.
2) Play a Low G.
3) Do a D gracenote while still on Low G.
4) Play a C.

E – Grip – D

1) Play an E.
2) Play a Low G.
3) Do a D gracenote while still on Low G.
4) Play a D.

E – Grip – E

1) Play an E.
2) Play a Low G.
3) Do a D gracenote while still on Low G.
4) Play an E.

E – Grip – F

1) Play an E.
2) Play a Low G.
3) Do a D gracenote while still on Low G.
4) Play an F.

E – Grip – High G

1) Play an E.
2) Play a Low G.
3) Do a D gracenote while still on Low G.
4) Play a High G.

E – Grip – High A

1) Play an E.
2) Play a Low G.
3) Do a D gracenote while still on Low G.
4) Play a High A.

F – Grip – Low A

1) Play an F.
2) Play a Low G.
3) Do a D gracenote while still on Low G.
4) Play a Low A.

F – Grip – B

1) Play an F.
2) Play a Low G.
3) Do a D gracenote while still on Low G.
4) Play a B.

F – Grip – C

1) Play an F.
2) Play a Low G.
3) Do a D gracenote while still on Low G.
4) Play a C.

F – Grip – D

1) Play an F.
2) Play a Low G.
3) Do a D gracenote while still on Low G.
4) Play a D.

F – Grip – E

1) Play an F.
2) Play a Low G.
3) Do a D gracenote while still on Low G.
4) Play an E.

F – Grip – F

1) Play an F.
2) Play a Low G.
3) Do a D gracenote while still on Low G.
4) Play an F.

F – Grip – High G

1) Play an F.
2) Play a Low G.
3) Do a D gracenote while still on Low G.
4) Play a High G.

F – Grip – High A

1) Play an F.
2) Play a Low G.
3) Do a D gracenote while still on Low G.
4) Play a High A.

High G – Grip – Low A

1) Play High G.
2) Play a Low G.
3) Do a D gracenote while still on Low G.
4) Play a Low A.

High G – Grip – B

1) Play High G.
2) Play a Low G.
3) Do a D gracenote while still on Low G.
4) Play a B.

High G – Grip – C

1) Play High G.
2) Play a Low G.
3) Do a D gracenote while still on Low G.
4) Play a C.

High G – Grip – D

1) Play High G.
2) Play a Low G.
3) Do a D gracenote while still on Low G.
4) Play a D.

High G – Grip – E

1) Play High G.
2) Play a Low G.
3) Do a D gracenote while still on Low G.
4) Play an E.

High G – Grip – F

1) Play High G.
2) Play a Low G.
3) Do a D gracenote while still on Low G.
4) Play an F.

High G – Grip – High G

1) Play High G.
2) Play a Low G.
3) Do a D gracenote while still on Low G.
4) Play a High G.

High G – Grip – High A

1) Play High G.
2) Play a Low G.
3) Do a D gracenote while still on Low G.
4) Play a High A.

High A – Grip – Low A

1) Play High A.
2) Play a Low G.
3) Do a D gracenote while still on Low G.
4) Play a Low A.

High A – Grip – B

1) Play High A.
2) Play a Low G.
3) Do a D gracenote while still on Low G.
4) Play a B.

High A – Grip – C

1) Play High A.
2) Play a Low G.
3) Do a D gracenote while still on Low G.
4) Play a C.

High A – Grip – D

1) Play High A.
2) Play a Low G.
3) Do a D gracenote while still on Low G.
4) Play a D.

High A – Grip – E

1) Play High A.
2) Play a Low G.
3) Do a D gracenote while still on Low G.
4) Play an E.

High A – Grip – F

1) Play High A.
2) Play a Low G.
3) Do a D gracenote while still on Low G.
4) Play an F.

High A – Grip – High G

1) Play High A.
2) Play a Low G.
3) Do a D gracenote while still on Low G.
4) Play a High G.

High A – Grip – High A
1) Play High A.
2) Play a Low G.
3) Do a D gracenote while still on Low G.
4) Play a High A.

The Grip can be played in between any note from Low A to High A.

Half Grip

Half Grip – Low A
1) Play Low G.
2) Do a D gracenote while still on Low G.
3) Play a Low A.

Half Grip – B
1) Play Low G.
2) Do a D gracenote while still on Low G.
3) Play a B.

Half Grip – C
1) Play Low G.
2) Do a D gracenote while still on Low G.
3) Play a C.

Half Grip – D
1) Play Low G.
2) Do a D gracenote while still on Low G.
3) Play a D.

Half Grip – E
1) Play Low G.
2) Do a D gracenote while still on Low G.
3) Play an E.

Half Grip – F
1) Play Low G.
2) Do a D gracenote while still on Low G.
3) Play an F.

Half Grip – High G

1) Play Low G.
2) Do a D gracenote while still on Low G.
3) Play a High G.

Half Grip – High A

1) Play Low G.
2) Do a D gracenote while still on Low G.
3) Play a High A.

The Half Grip always starts on a Low G and it can end on any note from Low G to High A.

B Grip

Low A – B Grip – Low A

1) Play Low A.
2) Play a Low G.
3) Do a B gracenote while still on Low G.
4) Play a Low A.

Low A – B Grip – B

1) Play Low A.
2) Play a Low G.
3) Do a B gracenote while still on Low G.
4) Play a B.

Low A – B Grip – C
  1) Play Low A.
  2) Play a Low G.
  3) Do a B gracenote while still on Low G.
  4) Play a C.

Low A – B Grip – D
  1) Play Low A.
  2) Play a Low G.
  3) Do a B gracenote while still on Low G.
  4) Play a D.

Low A – B Grip – E
  1) Play Low A.
  2) Play a Low G.
  3) Do a B gracenote while still on Low G.
  4) Play an E.

Low A – B Grip – F
  1) Play Low A.
  2) Play a Low G.
  3) Do a B gracenote while still on Low G.
  4) Play an F.

Low A – B Grip – High G
  1) Play Low A.
  2) Play a Low G.
  3) Do a B gracenote while still on Low G.
  4) Play a High G.

Low A – B Grip – High A
  1) Play Low A.
  2) Play a Low G.
  3) Do a B gracenote while still on Low G.
  4) Play a High A.

B – B Grip – Low A

1) Play a B.
2) Play a Low G.
3) Do a B gracenote while still on Low G.
4) Play a Low A.

B – B Grip – B

1) Play a B.
2) Play a Low G.
3) Do a B gracenote while still on Low G.
4) Play a B.

B – B Grip – C

1) Play a B.
2) Play a Low G.
3) Do a B gracenote while still on Low G.
4) Play a C.

B – B Grip – D

1) Play a B.
2) Play a Low G.
3) Do a B gracenote while still on Low G.
4) Play a D.

B – B Grip – E

1) Play a B.
2) Play a Low G.
3) Do a B gracenote while still on Low G.
4) Play an E.

B – B Grip – F

1) Play a B.
2) Play a Low G.
3) Do a B gracenote while still on Low G.
4) Play an F.

B – B Grip – High G

1) Play a B.
2) Play a Low G.
3) Do a B gracenote while still on Low G.
4) Play a High G.

B – B Grip – High A

1) Play a B.
2) Play a Low G.
3) Do a B gracenote while still on Low G.
4) Play a High A.

C – B Grip – Low A

1) Play a C.
2) Play a Low G.
3) Do a B gracenote while still on Low G.
4) Play a Low A.

C – B Grip – B

1) Play a C.
2) Play a Low G.
3) Do a B gracenote while still on Low G.
4) Play a B.

C – B Grip – C

1) Play a C.
2) Play a Low G.
3) Do a B gracenote while still on Low G.
4) Play a C.

C – B Grip – D

1) Play a C.
2) Play a Low G.
3) Do a B gracenote while still on Low G.
4) Play a D.

C – B Grip – E

1) Play a C.
2) Play a Low G.
3) Do a B gracenote while still on Low G.
4) Play an E.

C – B Grip – F

1) Play a C.
2) Play a Low G.
3) Do a B gracenote while still on Low G.
4) Play an F.

C – B Grip – High G

1) Play a C.
2) Play a Low G.
3) Do a B gracenote while still on Low G.
4) Play a High G.

C – B Grip – High A

1) Play a C.
2) Play a Low G.
3) Do a B gracenote while still on Low G.
4) Play a High A.

D – B Grip – Low A

1) Play a D.
2) Play a Low G.
3) Do a B gracenote while still on Low G.
4) Play a Low A.

D – B Grip – B

1) Play a D.
2) Play a Low G.
3) Do a B gracenote while still on Low G.
4) Play a B.

D – B Grip – C

1) Play a D.
2) Play a Low G.
3) Do a B gracenote while still on Low G.
4) Play a C.

D – B Grip – D

1) Play a D.
2) Play a Low G.
3) Do a B gracenote while still on Low G.
4) Play a D.

D – B Grip – E

1) Play a D.
2) Play a Low G.
3) Do a B gracenote while still on Low G.
4) Play an E.

D – B Grip – F

1) Play a D.
2) Play a Low G.
3) Do a B gracenote while still on Low G.
4) Play an F.

D – B Grip – High G

1) Play a D.
2) Play a Low G.
3) Do a B gracenote while still on Low G.
4) Play a High G.

D – B Grip – High A

1) Play a D.
2) Play a Low G.
3) Do a B gracenote while still on Low G.
4) Play a High A.

E – B Grip – Low A

1) Play an E.
2) Play a Low G.
3) Do a B gracenote while still on Low G.
4) Play a Low A.

E – B Grip – B

1) Play an E.
2) Play a Low G.
3) Do a B gracenote while still on Low G.
4) Play a B.

E – B Grip – C

1) Play an E.
2) Play a Low G.
3) Do a B gracenote while still on Low G.
4) Play a C.

E – B Grip – D

1) Play an E.
2) Play a Low G.
3) Do a B gracenote while still on Low G.
4) Play a D.

E – B Grip – E

1) Play an E.
2) Play a Low G.
3) Do a B gracenote while still on Low G.
4) Play an E.

E – B Grip – F

1) Play an E.
2) Play a Low G.
3) Do a B gracenote while still on Low G.
4) Play an F.

E – B Grip – High G

1) Play an E.
2) Play a Low G.
3) Do a B gracenote while still on Low G.
4) Play a High G.

E – B Grip – High A

1) Play an E.
2) Play a Low G.
3) Do a B gracenote while still on Low G.
4) Play a High A.

F – B Grip – Low A

1) Play an F.
2) Play a Low G.
3) Do a B gracenote while still on Low G.
4) Play a Low A.

F – B Grip – B

1) Play an F.
2) Play a Low G.
3) Do a B gracenote while still on Low G.
4) Play a B.

F – B Grip – C

1) Play an F.
2) Play a Low G.
3) Do a B gracenote while still on Low G.
4) Play a C.

F – B Grip – D

1) Play an F.
2) Play a Low G.
3) Do a B gracenote while still on Low G.
4) Play a D.

F – B Grip – E

1) Play an F.
2) Play a Low G.
3) Do a B gracenote while still on Low G.
4) Play an E.

F – B Grip – F

1) Play an F.
2) Play a Low G.
3) Do a B gracenote while still on Low G.
4) Play an F.

F – B Grip – High G

1) Play an F.
2) Play a Low G.
3) Do a B gracenote while still on Low G.
4) Play a High G.

F – B Grip – High A

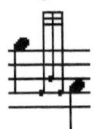
1) Play an F.
2) Play a Low G.
3) Do a B gracenote while still on Low G.
4) Play a High A.

High G – B Grip – Low A

1) Play High G.
2) Play a Low G.
3) Do a B gracenote while still on Low G.
4) Play a Low A.

High G – B Grip – B

1) Play High G.
2) Play a Low G.
3) Do a B gracenote while still on Low G.
4) Play a B.

High G – B Grip – C

1) Play High G.
2) Play a Low G.
3) Do a B gracenote while still on Low G.
4) Play a C.

High G – B Grip – D

1) Play High G.
2) Play a Low G.
3) Do a B gracenote while still on Low G.
4) Play a D.

High G – B Grip – E

1) Play High G.
2) Play a Low G.
3) Do a B gracenote while still on Low G.
4) Play an E.

High G – B Grip – F

1) Play High G.
2) Play a Low G.
3) Do a B gracenote while still on Low G.
4) Play an F.

High G – B Grip – High G

1) Play High G.
2) Play a Low G.
3) Do a B gracenote while still on Low G.
4) Play a High G.

High G – B Grip – High A

1) Play High G.
2) Play a Low G.
3) Do a B gracenote while still on Low G.
4) Play a High A.

High A – B Grip – Low A

1) Play High A.
2) Play a Low G.
3) Do a B gracenote while still on Low G.
4) Play a Low A.

High A – B Grip – B

1) Play High A.
2) Play a Low G.
3) Do a B gracenote while still on Low G.
4) Play a B.

High A – B Grip – C

1) Play High A.
2) Play a Low G.
3) Do a B gracenote while still on Low G.
4) Play a C.

High A – B Grip – D

1) Play High A.
2) Play a Low G.
3) Do a B gracenote while still on Low G.
4) Play a D.

High A – B Grip – E

1) Play High A.
2) Play a Low G.
3) Do a B gracenote while still on Low G.
4) Play an E.

High A – B Grip – F

1) Play High A.
2) Play a Low G.
3) Do a B gracenote while still on Low G.
4) Play an F.

High A – B Grip – High G

1) Play High A.
2) Play a Low G.
3) Do a B gracenote while still on Low G.
4) Play a High G.

High A – B Grip – High A

1) Play High A.
2) Play a Low G.
3) Do a B gracenote while still on Low G.
4) Play a High A.

The B Grip can be played in between any note from Low A to High A.

G Grip

G Grip to Low A

Low G – G Grip to Low A

1) Play Low G.
2) Do a G gracenote to Low A.
3) Play a Low G.
4) Do a D gracenote while still on Low G.
5) Play a Low A.

Low A – G Grip to Low A

1) Play Low A.
2) Do a G gracenote while on Low A.
3) Play a Low G.
4) Do a D gracenote while still on Low G.
5) Play a Low A.

B – G Grip to Low A

1) Play a B.
2) Do a G gracenote to Low A.
3) Play a Low G.
4) Do a D gracenote while still on Low G.
5) Play a Low A.

C – G Grip to Low A

1) Play a C.
2) Do a G gracenote to Low A.
3) Play a Low G.
4) Do a D gracenote while still on Low G.
5) Play a Low A.

D – G Grip to Low A

1) Play a D.
2) Do a G gracenote to Low A.
3) Play a Low G.
4) Do a D gracenote while still on Low G.
5) Play a Low A.

E – G Grip to Low A

1) Play an E.
2) Do a G gracenote to Low A.
3) Play a Low G.
4) Do a D gracenote while still on Low G.
5) Play a Low A.

F – G Grip to Low A

1) Play an F.
2) Do a G gracenote to Low A.
3) Play a Low G.
4) Do a D gracenote while still on Low G.
5) Play a Low A.

The G Grip to Low A can be played in between any note from Low G to F and it always ends on a Low A. The G Grip to Low A cannot be played any higher than an F.

G Grip to B

Low G – G Grip to B

1) Play Low G.
2) Do a G gracenote to B.
3) Play a Low G.
4) Do a D gracenote while still on Low G.
5) Play a B.

Low A – G Grip to B

1) Play Low A.
2) Do a G gracenote to B.
3) Play a Low G.
4) Do a D gracenote while still on Low G.
5) Play a B.

B – G Grip to B

1) Play a B.
2) Do a G gracenote while on B.
3) Play a Low G.
4) Do a D gracenote while still on Low G.
5) Play a B.

C – G Grip to B

1) Play a C.
2) Do a G gracenote to B.
3) Play a Low G.
4) Do a D gracenote while still on Low G.
5) Play a B.

D – G Grip to B

1) Play a D.
2) Do a G gracenote to B.
3) Play a Low G.
4) Do a D gracenote while still on Low G.
5) Play a B.

E – G Grip to B

1) Play an E.
2) Do a G gracenote to B.
3) Play a Low G.
4) Do a D gracenote while still on Low G.
5) Play a B.

F – G Grip to B

1) Play an F.
2) Do a G gracenote to B.
3) Play a Low G.
4) Do a D gracenote while still on Low G.
5) Play a B.

The G Grip to B can be played in between any note from Low G to F and it always ends on a B. The G Grip to B cannot be played any higher than an F.

G Grip to C

Low G – G Grip to C

1) Play Low G.
2) Do a G gracenote to C.
3) Play a Low G.
4) Do a D gracenote while still on Low G.
5) Play a C.

Low A – G Grip to C

    1) Play Low A.
    2) Do a G gracenote to C.
    3) Play a Low G.
    4) Do a D gracenote while still on Low G.
    5) Play a C.

B – G Grip to C

    1) Play a B.
    2) Do a G gracenote to C.
    3) Play a Low G.
    4) Do a D gracenote while still on Low G.
    5) Play a C.

C – G Grip to C

    1) Play a C.
    2) Do a G gracenote while on C.
    3) Play a Low G.
    4) Do a D gracenote while still on Low G.
    5) Play a C.

D – G Grip to C

    1) Play a D.
    2) Do a G gracenote to C.
    3) Play a Low G.
    4) Do a D gracenote while still on Low G.
    5) Play a C.

E – G Grip to C

    1) Play an E.
    2) Do a G gracenote to C.
    3) Play a Low G.
    4) Do a D gracenote while still on Low G.
    5) Play a C.

F – G Grip to C

1) Play an F.
2) Do a G gracenote to C.
3) Play a Low G.
4) Do a D gracenote while still on Low G.
5) Play a C.

The G Grip to C can be played in between any note from Low G to F and it always ends on a C. The G Grip to C cannot be played any higher than an F.

G Grip to D

Low G – G Grip to D

1) Play Low G.
2) Do a G gracenote to D.
3) Play a Low G.
4) Do a D gracenote while still on Low G.
5) Play a D.

Low A – G Grip to D

1) Play Low A.
2) Do a G gracenote to D.
3) Play a Low G.
4) Do a D gracenote while still on Low G.
5) Play a D.

B – G Grip to D

1) Play a B.
2) Do a G gracenote to D.
3) Play a Low G.
4) Do a D gracenote while still on Low G.
5) Play a D.

C – G Grip to D

1) Play a C.
2) Do a G gracenote to D.
3) Play a Low G.
4) Do a D gracenote while still on Low G.
5) Play a D.

D – G Grip to D

1) Play a D.
2) Do a G gracenote while on D.
3) Play a Low G.
4) Do a D gracenote while still on Low G.
5) Play a D.

E – G Grip to D

1) Play an E.
2) Do a G gracenote to D.
3) Play a Low G.
4) Do a D gracenote while still on Low G.
5) Play a D.

F – G Grip to D

1) Play an F.
2) Do a G gracenote to D.
3) Play a Low G.
4) Do a D gracenote while still on Low G.
5) Play a D.

The G Grip to D can be played in between any note from Low G to F and it always ends on a D. The G Grip to D cannot go any higher than an F.

G Grip to D with a B

Low G – G Grip to D with a B

1) Play Low G.
2) Do a G gracenote to D.
3) Play a Low G.
4) Do a B gracenote while still on Low G.
5) Play a D.

Low A – G Grip to D with a B

1) Play Low A.
2) Do a G gracenote to D.
3) Play a Low G.
4) Do a B gracenote while still on Low G.
5) Play a D.

B – G Grip to D with a B

1) Play a B.
2) Do a G gracenote to D.
3) Play a Low G.
4) Do a B gracenote while still on Low G.
5) Play a D.

C – G Grip to D with a B

1) Play a C.
2) Do a G gracenote to D.
3) Play a Low G.
4) Do a B gracenote while still on Low G.
5) Play a D.

D – G Grip to D with a B

1) Play a D.
2) Do a G gracenote while on D.
3) Play a Low G.
4) Do a B gracenote while still on Low G.
5) Play a D.

E – G Grip to D with a B

1) Play an E.
2) Do a G gracenote to D.
3) Play a Low G.
4) Do a B gracenote while still on Low G.
5) Play a D.

F – G Grip to D with a B

1) Play an F.
2) Do a G gracenote to D.
3) Play a Low G.
4) Do a B gracenote while still on Low G.
5) Play a D.

The G Grip to D with a B can be played in between any note from Low G to F and it always ends on a D. The G Grip to D with a B cannot be played any higher than a D.

G Grip to E

Low G – G Grip to E

1) Play Low G.
2) Do a G gracenote to E.
3) Play a Low G.
4) Do a D gracenote while still on Low G.
5) Play an E.

Low A – G Grip to E

1) Play Low A.
2) Do a G gracenote to E.
3) Play a Low G.
4) Do a D gracenote while still on Low G.
5) Play an E.

B – G Grip to E

1) Play a B.
2) Do a G gracenote to E.
3) Play a Low G.
4) Do a D gracenote while still on Low G.
5) Play an E.

C – G Grip to E

1) Play a C.
2) Do a G gracenote to E.
3) Play a Low G.
4) Do a D gracenote while still on Low G.
5) Play an E.

D – G Grip to E

1) Play a D.
2) Do a G gracenote to E.
3) Play a Low G.
4) Do a D gracenote while still on Low G.
5) Play an E.

E – G Grip to E

    1) Play an E.
    2) Do a G gracenote while on E.
    3) Play a Low G.
    4) Do a D gracenote while still on Low G.
    5) Play an E.

F – G Grip to E

    1) Play an F.
    2) Do a G gracenote to E.
    3) Play a Low G.
    4) Do a D gracenote while still on Low G.
    5) Play an E.

The G Grip to E can be played in between any note from Low G to F and it always ends on an E. The G Grip to E cannot go be played any higher than an F.

G Grip to F

Low G – G Grip to F

    1) Play Low G.
    2) Do a G gracenote to F.
    3) Play a Low G.
    4) Do an F gracenote while still on Low G.
    5) Play an F again.

Low A – G Grip to F

1) Play Low A.
2) Do a G gracenote to F.
3) Play a Low G.
4) Do an F gracenote while still on Low G.
5) Play an F again.

B – G Grip to F

1) Play a B.
2) Do a G gracenote to F.
3) Play a Low G.
4) Do an F gracenote while still on Low G.
5) Play an F again.

C – G Grip to F

1) Play a C.
2) Do a G gracenote to F.
3) Play a Low G.
4) Do an F gracenote while still on Low G.
5) Play an F again.

D – G Grip to F

1) Play a D.
2) Do a G gracenote to F.
3) Play a Low G.
4) Do an F gracenote while still on Low G.
5) Play an F again.

E – G Grip to F

1) Play an E.
2) Do a G gracenote to F.
3) Play a Low G.
4) Do an F gracenote while still on Low G.
5) Play an F again.

F – G Grip to F

1) Play an F.
2) Do a G gracenote while on F.
3) Play a Low G.
4) Do an F gracenote while still on Low G.
5) Play an F again.

The G Grip to F can be played in between any note from Low G to F and it always ends on an F. The G Grip to F cannot be played any higher than an F.

Thumb Grip

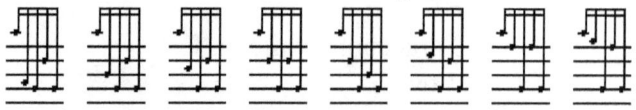

Thumb Grip to Low A

Low G – Thumb Grip to Low A

1) Play Low G.
2) Play a High A.
3) Play a Low A.
4) Play a Low G.
5) Do a D gracenote while still on Low G.
6) Play a Low A.

Low A – Thumb Grip to Low A

1) Play Low A.
2) Play a High A.
3) Play a Low A.
4) Play a Low G.
5) Do a D gracenote while still on Low G.
6) Play a Low A.

B – Thumb Grip to Low A

1) Play a B.
2) Play a High A.
3) Play a Low A.
4) Play a Low G.
5) Do a D gracenote while still on Low G.
6) Play a Low A.

C – Thumb Grip to Low A

1) Play a C.
2) Play a High A.
3) Play a Low A.
4) Play a Low G.
5) Do a D gracenote while still on Low G.
6) Play a Low A.

D – Thumb Grip to Low A

1) Play a D.
2) Play a High A.
3) Play a Low A.
4) Play a Low G.
5) Do a D gracenote while still on Low G.
6) Play a Low A.

E – Thumb Grip to Low A

1) Play an E.
2) Play a High A.
3) Play a Low A.
4) Play a Low G.
5) Do a D gracenote while still on Low G.
6) Play a Low A.

F – Thumb Grip to Low A

1) Play an F.
2) Play a High A.
3) Play a Low A.
4) Play a Low G.
5) Do a D gracenote while still on Low G.
6) Play a Low A.

High G – Thumb Grip to Low A

1) Play High G.
2) Play a High A.
3) Play a Low A.
4) Play a Low G.
5) Do a D gracenote while still on Low G.
6) Play a Low A.

The Thumb Grip to Low A can be played in between any note from Low G to high G and it always ends on a Low A. The Thumb Grip to Low A cannot be played any higher than High G.

Thumb Grip to B

Low G – Thumb Grip to B

1) Play Low G.
2) Play a High A.
3) Play a B.
4) Play a Low G.
5) Do a D gracenote while still on Low G.
6) Play a B.

Low A – Thumb Grip to B

1) Play Low A.
2) Play a High A.
3) Play a B.
4) Play a Low G.
5) Do a D gracenote while still on Low G.
6) Play a B.

B – Thumb Grip to B

1) Play a B.
2) Play a High A.
3) Play a B.
4) Play a Low G.
5) Do a D gracenote while still on Low G.
6) Play a B.

C – Thumb Grip to B

1) Play a C.
2) Play a High A.
3) Play a B.
4) Play a Low G.
5) Do a D gracenote while still on Low G.
6) Play a B.

D – Thumb Grip to B

1) Play a D.
2) Play a High A.
3) Play a B.
4) Play a Low G.
5) Do a D gracenote while still on Low G.
6) Play a B.

E – Thumb Grip to B

1) Play an E.
2) Play a High A.
3) Play a B.
4) Play a Low G.
5) Do a D gracenote while still on Low G.
6) Play a B.

F – Thumb Grip to B

1) Play an F.
2) Play a High A.
3) Play a B.
4) Play a Low G.
5) Do a D gracenote while still on Low G.
6) Play a B.

High G – Thumb Grip to B

1) Play High G.
2) Play a High A.
3) Play a B.
4) Play a Low G.
5) Do a D gracenote while still on Low G.
6) Play a B.

The Thumb Grip to B can be played in between any note from Low G to High G and it always ends on a B. The Thumb Grip to B cannot be played any higher than High G.

Thumb Grip to C

Low G – Thumb Grip to C

1) Play Low G.
2) Play a High A.
3) Play a C.
4) Play a Low G.
5) Do a D gracenote while still on Low G.
6) Play a C.

Low A – Thumb Grip to C
1) Play Low A.
2) Play a High A.
3) Play a C.
4) Play a Low G.
5) Do a D gracenote while still on Low G.
6) Play a C.

B – Thumb Grip to C
1) Play a B.
2) Play a High A.
3) Play a C.
4) Play a Low G.
5) Do a D gracenote while still on Low G.
6) Play a C.

C – Thumb Grip to C

1) Play a C.
2) Play a High A.
3) Play a C.
4) Play a Low G.
5) Do a D gracenote while still on Low G.
6) Play a C.

D – Thumb Grip to C
1) Play a D.
2) Play a High A.
3) Play a C.
4) Play a Low G.
5) Do a D gracenote while still on Low G.
6) Play a C.

E – Thumb Grip to C
1) Play an E.
2) Play a High A.
3) Play a C.
4) Play a Low G.
5) Do a D gracenote while still on Low G.
6) Play a C.

F – Thumb Grip to C
1) Play an F.
2) Play a High A.
3) Play a C.
4) Play a Low G.
5) Do a D gracenote while still on Low G.
6) Play a C.

High G – Thumb Grip to C
1) Play High G.
2) Play a High A.
3) Play a C.
4) Play a Low G.
5) Do a D gracenote while still on Low G.
6) Play a C.

The Thumb Grip to C can be played in between any note from Low G to High G and it always ends on a C. The Thumb Grip to C cannot be played any higher than High G.

Thumb Grip to D

Low G – Thumb Grip to D
    1) Play Low G.
    2) Play a High A.
    3) Play a D.
    4) Play a Low G.
    5) Do a D gracenote while still on Low G.
    6) Play a D.

Low A – Thumb Grip to D
    1) Play Low A.
    2) Play a High A.
    3) Play a D.
    4) Play a Low G.
    5) Do a D gracenote while still on Low G.
    6) Play a D.

B – Thumb Grip to D

    1) Play a B.
    2) Play a High A.
    3) Play a D.
    4) Play a Low G.
    5) Do a D gracenote while still on Low G.
    6) Play a D.

C – Thumb Grip to D
    1) Play a C.
    2) Play a High A.
    3) Play a D.
    4) Play a Low G.
    5) Do a D gracenote while still on Low G.
    6) Play a D.

D – Thumb Grip to D
1) Play a D.
2) Play a High A.
3) Play a D.
4) Play a Low G.
5) Do a D gracenote while still on Low G.
6) Play a D.

E – Thumb Grip to D
1) Play an E.
2) Play a High A.
3) Play a D.
4) Play a Low G.
5) Do a D gracenote while still on Low G.
6) Play a D.

F – Thumb Grip to D
1) Play an F.
2) Play a High A.
3) Play a D.
4) Play a Low G.
5) Do a D gracenote while still on Low G.
6) Play a D.

High G – Thumb Grip to D
1) Play High G.
2) Play a High A.
3) Play a D.
4) Play a Low G.
5) Do a D gracenote while still on Low G.
6) Play a D.

The Thumb Grip to D can be played in between any note from Low G to High G and it always ends on a D. The Thumb Grip to D cannot be played any higher than High G.

Thumb Grip to D with a B

Low G – Thumb Grip to D with a B
1) Play Low G.
2) Play a High A.
3) Play a D.
4) Play a Low G.
5) Do a B gracenote while still on Low G.
6) Play a D.

Low A – Thumb Grip to D with a B
1) Play Low A.
2) Play a High A.
3) Play a D.
4) Play a Low G.
5) Do a B gracenote while still on Low G.
6) Play a D.

B – Thumb Grip to D with a B
1) Play a B.
2) Play a High A.
3) Play a D.
4) Play a Low G.
5) Do a B gracenote while still on Low G.
6) Play a D.

C – *Thumb Grip to D with a B*
1) Play a C.
2) Play a High A.
3) Play a D.
4) Play a Low G.
5) Do a B gracenote while still on Low G.
6) Play a D.

D – *Thumb Grip to D with a B*
1) Play a D.
2) Play a High A.
3) Play a D.
4) Play a Low G.
5) Do a B gracenote while still on Low G.
6) Play a D.

E – *Thumb Grip to D with a B*
1) Play an E.
2) Play a High A.
3) Play a D.
4) Play a Low G.
5) Do a B gracenote while still on Low G.
6) Play a D.

F – *Thumb Grip to D with a B*
1) Play an F.
2) Play a High A.
3) Play a D.
4) Play a Low G.
5) Do a B gracenote while still on Low G.
6) Play a D.

High G – Thumb Grip to D with a B
1) Play High G.
2) Play a High A.
3) Play a D.
4) Play a Low G.
5) Do a B gracenote while still on Low G.
6) Play a D.

The Thumb Grip to D with a B can be played in between any note from Low G to High G and it always ends on a D. The Thumb Grip to D with a B cannot be played any higher than High G.

Thumb Grip to E

Low G – Thumb Grip to E
1) Play Low G.
2) Play a High A.
3) Play an E.
4) Play a Low G.
5) Do a D gracenote while still on Low G.
6) Play an E.

Low A – Thumb Grip to E
1) Play Low A.
2) Play a High A.
3) Play an E.
4) Play a Low G.
5) Do a D gracenote while still on Low G.
6) Play an E.

B – Thumb Grip to E
1) Play a B.
2) Play a High A.
3) Play an E.
4) Play a Low G.
5) Do a D gracenote while still on Low G.
6) Play an E.

C – Thumb Grip to E
1) Play a C.
2) Play a High A.
3) Play an E.
4) Play a Low G.
5) Do a D gracenote while still on Low G.
6) Play an E.

D – Thumb Grip to E

1) Play a D.
2) Play a High A.
3) Play an E.
4) Play a Low G.
5) Do a D gracenote while still on Low G.
6) Play an E.

E – Thumb Grip to E
1) Play an E.
2) Play a High A.
3) Play an E.
4) Play a Low G.
5) Do a D gracenote while still on Low G.
6) Play an E.

F – Thumb Grip to E
1) Play an F.
2) Play a High A.
3) Play an E.
4) Play a Low G.
5) Do a D gracenote while still on Low G.
6) Play an E.

High G – Thumb Grip to E
1) Play High G.
2) Play a High A.
3) Play an E.
4) Play a Low G.
5) Do a D gracenote while still on Low G.
6) Play an E.

The Thumb Grip to E can be played in between any note from Low G to High G and it always ends on an E. The Thumb Grip to E cannot be played any higher than High G.

Thumb Grip to F

Low G – Thumb Grip to F
    1) Play Low G.
    2) Play a High A.
    3) Play an F.
    4) Play a Low G.
    5) Do an F gracenote while still on Low G.
    6) Play an F.

Low A – Thumb Grip to F
    1) Play Low A.
    2) Play a High A.
    3) Play an F.
    4) Play a Low G.
    5) Do an F gracenote while still on Low G.
    6) Play an F.

B – Thumb Grip to F
    1) Play a B.
    2) Play a High A.
    3) Play an F.
    4) Play a Low G.
    5) Do an F gracenote while still on Low G.
    6) Play an F.

C – Thumb Grip to F
    1) Play a C.
    2) Play a High A.
    3) Play an F.
    4) Play a Low G.
    5) Do an F gracenote while still on Low G.
    6) Play an F.

D – Thumb Grip to F
1) Play a D.
2) Play a High A.
3) Play an F.
4) Play a Low G.
5) Do an F gracenote while still on Low G.
6) Play an F.

E – Thumb Grip to F
1) Play an E.
2) Play a High A.
3) Play an F.
4) Play a Low G.
5) Do an F gracenote while still on Low G.
6) Play an F.

F – Thumb Grip to F
1) Play an F.
2) Play a High A.
3) Play an F.
4) Play a Low G.
5) Do an F gracenote while still on Low G.
6) Play an F.

High G – Thumb Grip to F
1) Play High G.
2) Play a High A.
3) Play an F.
4) Play a Low G.
5) Do an F gracenote while still on Low G.
6) Play an F.

The Thumb Grip to F can be played in between note from Low G to High G and it always ends on an F. The Thumb Grip to E cannot be played any higher than High G.

Thumb Grip to High G

Low G – Thumb Grip to High G
    1) Play Low G.
    2) Play a High A.
    3) Play a High G.
    4) Play a Low G.
    5) Do an F gracenote while still on Low G.
    6) Play a High G.

Low A – Thumb Grip to High G
    1) Play Low A.
    2) Play a High A.
    3) Play a High G.
    4) Play a Low G.
    5) Do an F gracenote while still on Low G.
    6) Play a High G.

B – Thumb Grip to High G
    1) Play a B.
    2) Play a High A.
    3) Play a High G.
    4) Play a Low G.
    5) Do an F gracenote while still on Low G.
    6) Play a High G.

C – Thumb Grip to High G

1) Play a C.
2) Play a High A.
3) Play a High G.
4) Play a Low G.
5) Do an F gracenote while still on Low G.
6) Play a High G.

D – Thumb Grip to High G

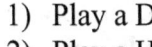
1) Play a D.
2) Play a High A.
3) Play a High G.
4) Play a Low G.
5) Do an F gracenote while still on Low G.
6) Play a High G.

E – Thumb Grip to High G

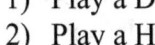
1) Play an E.
2) Play a High A.
3) Play a High G.
4) Play a Low G.
5) Do an F gracenote while still on Low G.
6) Play a High G.

F – Thumb Grip to High G

1) Play an F.
2) Play a High A.
3) Play a High G.
4) Play a Low G.
5) Do an F gracenote while still on Low G.
6) Play a High G.

High G – Thumb Grip to High G

1) Play High G.
2) Play a High A.
3) Play a High G.
4) Play a Low G.
5) Do an F gracenote while still on Low G.
6) Play a High G.

The Thumb Grip to High G can be played in between any note from Low G to High G and it always ends on a High G. The Thumb Grip to High G cannot be played any higher than High G.

Half Grip

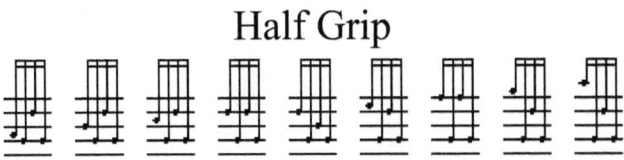

Half Grip to Low A

High G – Half Grip to Low A

1) Play High A.
2) Play a Low A.
3) Play a Low G.
4) Do a D gracenote while still on Low G.
5) Play a Low A.

The Half Grip to Low A is usually only played from a High A but it always ends on a Low A.

Half Grip to B

High A – Half Grip to B

1) Play High A.
2) Play a B.
3) Play a Low G.
4) Do a D gracenote while still on Low G.
5) Play a B.

The Half Grip to B is usually only played from a High A but it always ends on a B.

Half Grip to C

High A – Half Grip to C

    1) Play High A.
    2) Play a C.
    3) Play a Low G.
    4) Do a D gracenote while still on Low G.
    5) Play a C.

The Half Grip to C is usually only played from a High A but it always ends on a C.

Half Grip to D

High A – Half Grip to D
    1) Play High A.
    2) Play a D.
    3) Play a Low G.
    4) Do a D gracenote while still on Low G.
    5) Play a D.

The Half Grip to D is usually only played from a High A but it always ends on a D.

Half Grip to D with a B

High A – Half Grip to D with a B

1) Play High A.
2) Play a D.
3) Play a Low G.
4) Do a B gracenote while still on Low G.
5) Play a D.

The Half Grip to D with a B is usually only played from a High A but it always ends on a D.

Half Grip to E

High A – Half Grip to E

      1) Play a High A.
      2) Play an E.
      3) Play a Low G.
      4) Do a D gracenote while still on Low G.
      5) Play an E.

The Half Grip to E is usually only played from a High A but it always ends on an E.

Half Grip to F

High A – Half Grip to F

      1) Play High A.
      2) Play an F.
      3) Play a Low G.
      4) Do an F gracenote while still on Low G.
      5) Play an F.

The Half Grip to F is usually only played from a High A but it always ends on an F.

Half Grip to High G

Low A – Half Grip to High G

1) Play Low A.
2) Do a G gracenote to Low G.
3) Do a D gracenote while still on Low G.
4) Play a High G.

B – Half Grip to High G

1) Play a B.
2) Do a G gracenote to Low G.
3) Do a D gracenote while still on Low G.
4) Play a High G.

C – Half Grip to High G

1) Play a C.
2) Do a G gracenote to Low G.
3) Do a D gracenote while still on Low G.
4) Play a High G.

D – Half Grip to High G

1) Play a D.
2) Do a G gracenote to Low G.
3) Do a D gracenote while still on Low G.
4) Play a High G.

E – Half Grip to High G

1) Play an E.
2) Do a G gracenote to Low G.
3) Do a D gracenote while still on Low G.
4) Play a High G.

F – Half Grip to High G

1) Play an F.
2) Do a G gracenote while still on Low G.
3) Do a D gracenote while still on Low G.
4) Play a High G.

The Half Grip to High G can be played in between any note from Low A to F and it always ends on High G. The Half Grip to High G cannot be played any higher than an F.

Half Grip to High A

Low A – Half Grip to High A

1) Play Low A.
2) Play a High A.
3) Play a Low G.
4) Do a D gracenote while still on Low G.
5) Play a High A.

B – Half Grip to High A

1) Play a B.
2) Play a High A.
3) Play a Low G.
4) Do a D gracenote while still on Low G.
5) Play a High A.

C – Half Grip to High A

1) Play a C.
2) Play a High A.
3) Play a Low G.
4) Do a D gracenote while still on Low G.
5) Play a High A.

D – Half Grip to High A

1) Play a D.
2) Play a High A.
3) Play a Low G.
4) Do a D gracenote while still on Low G.
5) Play a High A.

E – Half Grip to High A

1) Play an E.
2) Play a High A.
3) Play a Low G.
4) Do a D gracenote while still on Low G.
5) Play a High A.

F – Half Grip to High A

1) Play an F.
2) Play a High A.
3) Play a Low G.
4) Do a D gracenote while still on Low G.
5) Play a High A.

High G – Half Grip to High A

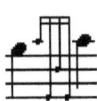
1) Play High G.
2) Play a High A.
3) Play a Low G.
4) Do a D gracenote while still on Low G.
5) Play a High A.

The Half Grip to High A can be played in between any note from Low A to High G and it always ends on a High A.

Tachum

The Tachum is a group of notes and not a single embellishment. The C note is short and the Low A is held because of the dot that follows it. When played correctly it will make a 'Tach-um' sound.

Low G – Tachum

1) Play Low G.
2) Do a G gracenote to a C.
3) Do a D gracenote to Low A.

Low A – Tachum

1) Play Low A.
2) Do a G gracenote to a C.
3) Do a D gracenote to Low A.

B – Tachum

1) Play a B.
2) Do a G gracenote to a C.
3) Do a D gracenote to Low A.

C – Tachum

1) Play a C.
2) Do a G gracenote to a C.
3) Do a D gracenote to Low A.

D – Tachum

1) Play a D.
2) Do a G gracenote to a C.
3) Do a D gracenote to Low A.

E – Tachum

1) Play an E.
2) Do a G gracenote to a C.
3) Do a D gracenote to Low A.

F – Tachum

1) Play an F.
2) Do a G gracenote to a C.
3) Do a D gracenote to Low A.

The Tachum can be played in between any note from Low G to F.

Birls

A Birl is played by striking the Low A finger across the Low A hole twice, sounding two quick Low G's. The traditional way is to strike the finger down and then across from left to right (while holding the chanter) making a "7" motion across the hole. You can also strike it twice by going left to right called a cobra strike or you can double tap the Low A hole.

Birl

Low A – Birl

1) Play Low A.
2) Strike your Low A finger twice to sound two quick Low G's forming a Low A.

B – Birl

1) Play a B.
2) Strike your Low A finger twice to sound two quick Low G's forming a Low A.

C – Birl

1) Play a C.
2) Strike your Low A finger twice to sound two quick Low G's forming a Low A.

D – Birl

1) Play a D.
2) Strike your Low A finger twice to sound two quick Low G's forming a Low A.

E – Birl

1) Play an E.
2) Strike your Low A finger twice to sound two quick Low G's forming a Low A.

F – Birl

1) Play an F.
2) Strike your Low A finger twice to sound two quick Low G's forming a Low A.

High G – Birl

1) Play High G.
2) Strike your Low A finger twice to sound two quick Low G's forming a Low A.

High A – Birl

1) Play High A.
2) Strike your Low A finger twice to sound two quick Low G's forming a Low A.

A Birl can be played in between any note from Low A to High A and it always ends on a Low A.

A Birl

Low A – A Birl

1) Play Low A.
2) Strike your Low A finger twice to sound two quick Low G's forming a Low A.

B – A Birl

1) Play a B.
2) Play Low A and then strike your Low A finger twice to sound two quick Low G's forming a Low A.

C – A Birl

1) Play a C.
2) Play Low A and then strike your Low A finger twice to sound two quick Low G's forming a Low A.

D – A Birl

1) Play a D.
2) Play Low A and then strike your Low A finger twice to sound two quick Low G's forming a Low A.

E – A Birl

1) Play an E.
2) Play Low A and then strike your Low A finger twice to sound two quick Low G's forming a Low A.

F – A Birl

1) Play an F.
2) Play Low A and then strike your Low A finger twice to sound two quick Low G's forming a Low A.

High G – A Birl

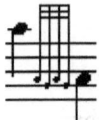
1) Play High G.
2) Play Low A and then strike your Low A finger twice to sound two quick Low G's forming a Low A.

High A – A Birl

1) Play High A.
2) Play Low A and then strike your Low A finger twice to sound two quick Low G's forming a Low A.

The A Birl can be played in between any note from B to High A and it always ends on a Low A.

G Birl

Low A – G Birl

1) Play Low A.
2) Do a G gracenote while on Low A.
3) Strike your Low A finger twice to sound two quick Low G's forming a Low A.

B – G Birl

1) Play a B.
2) Do a G gracenote to Low A.
3) Strike your Low A finger twice to sound two quick Low G's forming a Low A.

C – G Birl

1) Play a C.
2) Do a G gracenote to Low A.
3) Strike your Low A finger twice to sound two quick Low G's forming a Low A.

D – G Birl

1) Play a D.
2) Do a G gracenote to Low A.
3) Strike your Low A finger twice to sound two quick Low G's forming a Low A.

E – G Birl

1) Play an E.
2) Do a G gracenote to Low A.
3) Strike your Low A finger twice to sound two quick Low G's forming a Low A.

F – G Birl

1) Play an F.
2) Do a G gracenote to Low A.
3) Strike your Low A finger twice to sound two quick Low G's forming a Low A.

The G Birl can be played in between any note from Low A to F and it always ends on a Low A.

Thumb Birl

Low A – Thumb Birl

1) Play Low A.
2) Play a High A.
3) Play Low A and then strike your Low A finger twice to sound two quick Low G's forming a Low A.

B – Thumb Birl

1) Play a B.
2) Play a High A.
3) Play Low A and then strike your Low A finger twice to sound two quick Low G's forming a Low A.

C – Thumb Birl

1) Play a C.
2) Play a High A.
3) Play Low A and then strike your Low A finger twice to sound two quick Low G's forming a Low A.

D – Thumb Birl

1) Play a D.
2) Play a High A.
3) Play Low A and then strike your Low A finger twice to sound two quick Low G's forming a Low A.

E – Thumb Birl

1) Play an E.
2) Play a High A.
3) Play Low A and then strike your Low A finger twice to sound two quick Low G's forming a Low A.

F – Thumb Birl

1) Play an F.
2) Play a High A.
3) Play Low A and then strike your Low A finger twice to sound two quick Low G's forming a Low A.

High G – Thumb Birl

1) Play High G.
2) Play a High A.
3) Play Low A and then strike your Low A finger twice to sound two quick Low G's forming a Low A.

The Thumb Birl can be played in between any note from Low A to High G and it always ends on a Low A.

Taorluaths

Taorluath

Low A – Taorluath – Low A

    1) Play Low A.
    2) Play a Low G.
    3) Do a D gracenote while still on Low G.
    4) Do an E gracenote to Low A.

Low A – Taorluath – B

    1) Play Low A.
    2) Play a Low G.
    3) Do a D gracenote while still on Low G.
    4) Do an E gracenote to B.

Low A – Taorluath – C

    1) Play Low A.
    2) Play a Low G.
    3) Do a D gracenote while still on Low G.
    4) Do an E gracenote to C.

Low A – Taorluath – D

    1) Play Low A.
    2) Play a Low G.
    3) Do a D gracenote while still on Low G.
    4) Do an E gracenote to C.

B – Taorluath – Low A

    1) Play a B.
    2) Play a Low G.
    3) Do a D gracenote while still on Low G.
    4) Do an E gracenote to Low A.

B – Taorluath – B

1) Play a B.
2) Play a Low G.
3) Do a D gracenote while still on Low G.
4) Do an E gracenote to B.

B – Taorluath – C

1) Play a B.
2) Play a Low G.
3) Do a D gracenote while still on Low G.
4) Do an E gracenote to C.

B – Taorluath – D

1) Play a B.
2) Play a Low G.
3) Do a D gracenote while still on Low G.
4) Do an E gracenote to C.

C – Taorluath – Low A

1) Play a C.
2) Play a Low G.
3) Do a D gracenote while still on Low G.
4) Do an E gracenote to Low A.

C – Taorluath – B

1) Play a C.
2) Play a Low G.
3) Do a D gracenote while still on Low G.
4) Play an E gracenote to B.

C – Taorluath – C

1) Play a C.
2) Play a Low G.
3) Do a D gracenote while still on Low G.
4) Play an E gracenote to C.

C – Taorluath – D

1) Play a C.
2) Play a Low G.
3) Do a D gracenote while still on Low G.
4) Play an E gracenote to C.

D – Taorluath – Low A

1) Play a D.
2) Play a Low G.
3) Do a D gracenote while still on Low G.
4) Do an E gracenote to Low A.

D – Taorluath – B

1) Play a D.
2) Play a Low G.
3) Do a D gracenote while still on Low G.
4) Do an E gracenote to B.

D – Taorluath – C

1) Play a D.
2) Play a Low G.
3) Do a D gracenote while still on Low G.
4) Do an E gracenote to C.

D – Taorluath – D

1) Play a D.
2) Play a Low G.
3) Do a D gracenote while still on Low G.
4) Do an E gracenote to D.

E – Taorluath – Low A

1) Play an E.
2) Play a Low G.
3) Do a D gracenote while still on Low G.
4) Do an E gracenote to Low A.

E – Taorluath – B

1) Play an E.
2) Play a Low G.
3) Do a D gracenote while still on Low G.
4) Do an E gracenote to Low A.

E – Taorluath – C

1) Play an E.
2) Play a Low G.
3) Do a D gracenote while still on Low G.
4) Do an E gracenote to C.

E – Taorluath – D

1) Play an E.
2) Play a Low G.
3) Do a D gracenote while still on Low G.
4) Do an E gracenote to D.

F – Taorluath – Low A

1) Play an F.
2) Play a Low G.
3) Do a D gracenote while still on Low G.
4) Do an E gracenote to Low A.

F – Taorluath – B

1) Play an F.
2) Play a Low G.
3) Do a D gracenote while still on Low G.
4) Do an E gracenote to B.

F – Taorluath – C

1) Play an F.
2) Play a Low G.
3) Do a D gracenote while still on Low G.
4) Do an E gracenote to C.

F – Taorluath – D

1) Play an F.
2) Play a Low G.
3) Do a D gracenote while still on Low G.
4) Do an E gracenote to D.

High G – Taorluath – Low A

1) Play High G.
2) Play a Low G.
3) Do a D gracenote while still on Low G.
4) Do an E gracenote to Low A.

High G – Taorluath – B

1) Play High G.
2) Play a Low G.
3) Do a D gracenote while still on Low G.
4) Do an E gracenote to B.

High G – Taorluath – C

1) Play High G.
2) Play a Low G.
3) Do a D gracenote while still on Low G.
4) Do an E gracenote to C.

High G – Taorluath – D

1) Play High G.
2) Play a Low G.
3) Do a D gracenote while still on Low G.
4) Do an E gracenote to D.

High A – Taorluath – Low A

1) Play High A.
2) Play a Low G.
3) Do a D gracenote while still on Low G.
4) Do an E gracenote to Low A.

High A – Taorluath – B

1) Play High A.
2) Play a Low G.
3) Do a D gracenote while still on Low G.
4) Do an E gracenote to B.

High A – Taorluath – C

1) Play High A.
2) Play a Low G.
3) Do a D gracenote while still on Low G.
4) Do an E gracenote to C.

High A – Taorluath – D

1) Play High A.
2) Play a Low G.
3) Do a D gracenote while still on Low G.
4) Do an E gracenote to D.

The Taorluath can be played in between any note from Low A to High A and it always ends on a note in between Low A and D.

B Taorluath

Low A – B Taorluath – Low A

1) Play Low A.
2) Play a Low G.
3) Do a B gracenote while still on Low G.
4) Do an E gracenote to Low A.

Low A – B Taorluath – B

1) Play Low A.
2) Play a Low G.
3) Do a B gracenote while still on Low G.
4) Do an E gracenote to B.

Low A – B Taorluath – C

1) Play Low A.
2) Play a Low G.
3) Do a B gracenote while still on Low G.
4) Do an E gracenote to C.

Low A – B Taorluath – D

1) Play Low A.
2) Play a Low G.
3) Do a B gracenote while still on Low G.
4) Do an E gracenote to D.

B – B Taorluath – Low A

1) Play a B.
2) Play a Low G.
3) Do a B gracenote while still on Low G.
4) Do an E gracenote to Low A.

B – B Taorluath – B

1) Play a B.
2) Play a Low G.
3) Do a B gracenote while still on Low G.
4) Do an E gracenote to B.

B – B Taorluath – C

1) Play a B.
2) Play a Low G.
3) Do a B gracenote while still on Low G.
4) Do an E gracenote to C.

B – B Taorluath – D

1) Play a B.
2) Play a Low G.
3) Do a B gracenote while still on Low G.
4) Do an E gracenote to D.

C – B Taorluath – Low A

1) Play a C.
2) Play a Low G.
3) Do a B gracenote while still on Low G.
4) Do an E gracenote to Low A.

C – B Taorluath – B

1) Play a C.
2) Play a Low G.
3) Do a B gracenote while still on Low G.
4) Do an E gracenote to B.

C – B Taorluath – C

1) Play a C.
2) Play a Low G.
3) Do a B gracenote while still on Low G.
4) Do an E gracenote to C.

C – B Taorluath – D

1) Play a C.
2) Play a Low G.
3) Do a B gracenote while still on Low G.
4) Do an E gracenote to D.

D – B Taorluath – Low A

1) Play a D.
2) Play a Low G.
3) Do a B gracenote while still on Low G.
4) Do an E gracenote to Low A.

D – B Taorluath – B

1) Play a D.
2) Play a Low G.
3) Do a B gracenote while still on Low G.
4) Do an E gracenote to B.

D – B Taorluath – C

1) Play a D.
2) Play a Low G.
3) Do a B gracenote while still on Low G.
4) Do an E gracenote to C.

D – B Taorluath – D

1) Play a D.
2) Play a Low G.
3) Do a B gracenote while still on Low G.
4) Do an E gracenote to D.

E – B Taorluath – Low A

1) Play an E.
2) Play a Low G.
3) Do a B gracenote while still on Low G.
4) Do an E gracenote to Low A.

E – B Taorluath – B

1) Play an E.
2) Play a Low G.
3) Do a B gracenote while still on Low G.
4) Do an E gracenote to B.

E – B Taorluath – C

1) Play an E.
2) Play a Low G.
3) Do a B gracenote while still on Low G.
4) Do an E gracenote to C.

E – B Taorluath – D

1) Play an E.
2) Play a Low G.
3) Do a B gracenote while still on Low G.
4) Do an E gracenote to D.

F – B Taorluath – Low A

1) Play an F.
2) Play a Low G.
3) Do a B gracenote while still on Low G.
4) Do an E gracenote to Low A.

F – B Taorluath – B

1) Play an F.
2) Play a Low G.
3) Do a B gracenote while still on Low G.
4) Do an E gracenote to B.

F – B Taorluath – C

1) Play an F.
2) Play a Low G.
3) Do a B gracenote while still on Low G.
4) Do an E gracenote to C.

F – B Taorluath – D

1) Play an F.
2) Play a Low G.
3) Do a B gracenote while still on Low G.
4) Do an E gracenote to D.

High G – B Taorluath – Low A

1) Play High G.
2) Play a Low G.
3) Do a B gracenote while still on Low G.
4) Do an E gracenote to Low A.

High G – B Taorluath – B

1) Play High G.
2) Play a Low G.
3) Do a B gracenote while still on Low G.
4) Do an E gracenote to B.

High G – B Taorluath – C

1) Play High G.
2) Play a Low G.
3) Do a B gracenote while still on Low G.
4) Do an E gracenote to C.

High G – B Taorluath – D

1) Play High G.
2) Play a Low G.
3) Do a B gracenote while still on Low G.
4) Do an E gracenote to D.

High A – B Taorluath – Low A

1) Play High A.
2) Play a Low G.
3) Do a B gracenote while still on Low G.
4) Do an E gracenote to Low A.

High A – B Taorluath – B

1) Play High A.
2) Play a Low G.
3) Do a B gracenote while still on Low G.
4) Do an E gracenote to B.

High A – B Taorluath – C

1) Play High A.
2) Play a Low G.
3) Do a B gracenote while still on Low G.
4) Do an E gracenote to C.

High A – B Taorluath – D

1) Play High A.
2) Play a Low G.
3) Do a B gracenote while still on Low G.
4) Do an E gracenote to D.

The B Taorluath can be played after any note from Low A to High A and it always ends on a note in between Low A and D.

Bublys

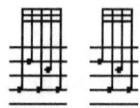

Bubly

Low A – Bubly – Low A
1) Play Low A.
2) Play a Low G.
3) Do a D gracenote while on Low G.
4) Do a C gracenote while still on Low G.
5) Play Low A.

Low A – Bubly – B
1) Play Low A.
2) Play a Low G.
3) Do a D gracenote while on Low G.
4) Do a C gracenote while still on Low G.
5) Play a B.

Low A – Bubly – C
1) Play Low A.
2) Play a Low G.
3) Do a D gracenote while on Low G.
4) Do a C gracenote while still on Low G.
5) Play a C.

Low A – Bubly – D
1) Play Low A.
2) Play a Low G.
3) Do a D gracenote while on Low G.
4) Do a C gracenote while still on Low G.
5) Play a D.

Low A – Bubly – E

1) Play Low A.
2) Play a Low G.
3) Do a D gracenote while on Low G.
4) Do a C gracenote while still on Low G.
5) Play an E.

Low A – Bubly – F

1) Play Low A.
2) Play a Low G.
3) Do a D gracenote while on Low G.
4) Do a C gracenote while still on Low G.
5) Play an F.

Low A – Bubly – High G

1) Play Low A.
2) Play a Low G.
3) Do a D gracenote while on Low G.
4) Do a C gracenote while still on Low G.
5) Play High G.

Low A – Bubly – High A

1) Play Low A.
2) Play a Low G.
3) Do a D gracenote while on Low G.
4) Do a C gracenote while still on Low G.
5) Play High A.

B – Bubly – Low A

1) Play a B.
2) Play a Low G.
3) Do a D gracenote while on Low G.
4) Do a C gracenote while still on Low G.
5) Play Low A.

B – Bubly – B

1) Play a B.
2) Play a Low G.
3) Do a D gracenote while on Low G.
4) Do a C gracenote while still on Low G.
5) Play a B.

B – Bubly – C

1) Play a B.
2) Play a Low G.
3) Do a D gracenote while on Low G.
4) Do a C gracenote while still on Low G.
5) Play a C.

B – Bubly – D

1) Play a B.
2) Play a Low G.
3) Do a D gracenote while on Low G.
4) Do a C gracenote while still on Low G.
5) Play a D.

B – Bubly – E

1) Play a B.
2) Play a Low G.
3) Do a D gracenote while on Low G.
4) Do a C gracenote while still on Low G.
5) Play an E.

B – Bubly – F

1) Play a B.
2) Play a Low G.
3) Do a D gracenote while on Low G.
4) Do a C gracenote while still on Low G.
5) Play an F.

B – Bubly – High G

   1) Play a B.
   2) Play a Low G.
   3) Do a D gracenote while on Low G.
   4) Do a C gracenote while still on Low G.
   5) Play High G.

B – Bubly – High A

   1) Play a B.
   2) Play a Low G.
   3) Do a D gracenote while on Low G.
   4) Do a C gracenote while still on Low G.
   5) Play High A.

C – Bubly – Low A

   1) Play a C.
   2) Play a Low G.
   3) Do a D gracenote while on Low G.
   4) Do a C gracenote while still on Low G.
   5) Play Low A.

C – Bubly – B

   1) Play a C.
   2) Play a Low G.
   3) Do a D gracenote while on Low G.
   4) Do a C gracenote while still on Low G.
   5) Play a B.

C – Bubly – C

   1) Play a C.
   2) Play a Low G.
   3) Do a D gracenote while on Low G.
   4) Do a C gracenote while still on Low G.
   5) Play a C.

C – Bubly – D

1) Play a C.
2) Play a Low G.
3) Do a D gracenote while on Low G.
4) Do a C gracenote while still on Low G.
5) Play a D.

C – Bubly – E

1) Play a C.
2) Play a Low G.
3) Do a D gracenote while on Low G.
4) Do a C gracenote while still on Low G.
5) Play an E.

C – Bubly – F

1) Play a C.
2) Play a Low G.
3) Do a D gracenote while on Low G.
4) Do a C gracenote while still on Low G.
5) Play an F.

C – Bubly – High G

1) Play a C.
2) Play a Low G.
3) Do a D gracenote while on Low G.
4) Do a C gracenote while still on Low G.
5) Play High G.

C – Bubly – High A

1) Play a C.
2) Play a Low G.
3) Do a D gracenote while on Low G.
4) Do a C gracenote while still on Low G.
5) Play High A.

D – Bubly – Low A

1) Play a D.
2) Play a Low G.
3) Do a D gracenote while on Low G.
4) Do a C gracenote while still on Low G.
5) Play Low A.

D – Bubly – B

1) Play a D.
2) Play a Low G.
3) Do a D gracenote while on Low G.
4) Do a C gracenote while still on Low G.
5) Play a B.

D – Bubly – C

1) Play a D.
2) Play a Low G.
3) Do a D gracenote while on Low G.
4) Do a C gracenote while still on Low G.
5) Play a C.

D – Bubly – D

1) Play a D.
2) Play a Low G.
3) Do a D gracenote while on Low G.
4) Do a C gracenote while still on Low G.
5) Play a D.

D – Bubly – E

1) Play a D.
2) Play a Low G.
3) Do a D gracenote while on Low G.
4) Do a C gracenote while still on Low G.
5) Play an E.

D – Bubly – F

1) Play a D.
2) Play a Low G.
3) Do a D gracenote while on Low G.
4) Do a C gracenote while still on Low G.
5) Play an F.

D – Bubly – High G

1) Play a D.
2) Play a Low G.
3) Do a D gracenote while on Low G.
4) Do a C gracenote while still on Low G.
5) Play High G.

D – Bubly – High A

1) Play a D.
2) Play a Low G.
3) Do a D gracenote while on Low G.
4) Do a C gracenote while still on Low G.
5) Play High A.

E – Bubly – Low A

1) Play an E.
2) Play a Low G.
3) Do a D gracenote while on Low G.
4) Do a C gracenote while still on Low G.
5) Play Low A.

E – Bubly – B

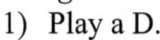
1) Play an E.
2) Play a Low G.
3) Do a D gracenote while on Low G.
4) Do a C gracenote while still on Low G.
5) Play a B.

E – Bubly – C

1) Play an E.
2) Play a Low G.
3) Do a D gracenote while on Low G.
4) Do a C gracenote while still on Low G.
5) Play a C.

E – Bubly – D

1) Play an E.
2) Play a Low G.
3) Do a D gracenote while on Low G.
4) Do a C gracenote while still on Low G.
5) Play a D.

E – Bubly – E

1) Play an E.
2) Play a Low G.
3) Do a D gracenote while on Low G.
4) Do a C gracenote while still on Low G.
5) Play an E.

E – Bubly – F

1) Play an E.
2) Play a Low G.
3) Do a D gracenote while on Low G.
4) Do a C gracenote while still on Low G.
5) Play an F.

E – Bubly – High G

1) Play an E.
2) Play a Low G.
3) Do a D gracenote while on Low G.
4) Do a C gracenote while still on Low G.
5) Play High G.

E – Bubly – High A

1) Play an E.
2) Play a Low G.
3) Do a D gracenote while on Low G.
4) Do a C gracenote while still on Low G.
5) Play High A.

F – Bubly – Low A

1) Play an F.
2) Play a Low G.
3) Do a D gracenote while on Low G.
4) Do a C gracenote while still on Low G.
5) Play Low A.

F – Bubly – B

1) Play an F.
2) Play a Low G.
3) Do a D gracenote while on Low G.
4) Do a C gracenote while still on Low G.
5) Play a B.

F – Bubly – C

1) Play an F.
2) Play a Low G.
3) Do a D gracenote while on Low G.
4) Do a C gracenote while still on Low G.
5) Play a C.

F – Bubly – D

1) Play an F.
2) Play a Low G.
3) Do a D gracenote while on Low G.
4) Do a C gracenote while still on Low G.
5) Play a D.

F – Bubly – E

1) Play an F.
2) Play a Low G.
3) Do a D gracenote while on Low G.
4) Do a C gracenote while still on Low G.
5) Play an E.

F – Bubly – F

1) Play an F.
2) Play a Low G.
3) Do a D gracenote while on Low G.
4) Do a C gracenote while still on Low G.
5) Play an F.

F – Bubly – High G

1) Play an F.
2) Play a Low G.
3) Do a D gracenote while on Low G.
4) Do a C gracenote while still on Low G.
5) Play High G.

F – Bubly – High A

1) Play an F.
2) Play a Low G.
3) Do a D gracenote while on Low G.
4) Do a C gracenote while still on Low G.
5) Play High A.

High G – Bubly – Low A

1) Play High G.
2) Play a Low G.
3) Do a D gracenote while on Low G.
4) Do a C gracenote while still on Low G.
5) Play Low A.

High G – Bubly – B

1) Play High G.
2) Play a Low G.
3) Do a D gracenote while on Low G.
4) Do a C gracenote while still on Low G.
5) Play a B.

High G – Bubly – C

1) Play High G.
2) Play a Low G.
3) Do a D gracenote while on Low G.
4) Do a C gracenote while still on Low G.
5) Play a C.

High G – Bubly – D

1) Play High G.
2) Play a Low G.
3) Do a D gracenote while on Low G.
4) Do a C gracenote while still on Low G.
5) Play a D.

High G – Bubly – E

1) Play High G.
2) Play a Low G.
3) Do a D gracenote while on Low G.
4) Do a C gracenote while still on Low G.
5) Play an E.

High G – Bubly – F

1) Play High G.
2) Play a Low G.
3) Do a D gracenote while on Low G.
4) Do a C gracenote while still on Low G.
5) Play an F.

High G – Bubly – High G
1) Play High G.
2) Play a Low G.
3) Do a D gracenote while on Low G.
4) Do a C gracenote while still on Low G.
5) Play High G.

High G – Bubly – High A
1) Play High G.
2) Play a Low G.
3) Do a D gracenote while on Low G.
4) Do a C gracenote while still on Low G.
5) Play High A.

High A – Bubly – Low A

1) Play High A.
2) Play a Low G.
3) Do a D gracenote while on Low G.
4) Do a C gracenote while still on Low G.
5) Play Low A.

High A – Bubly – B

1) Play High A.
2) Play a Low G.
3) Do a D gracenote while on Low G.
4) Do a C gracenote while still on Low G.
5) Play a B.

High A – Bubly – C
1) Play High A.
2) Play a Low G.
3) Do a D gracenote while on Low G.
4) Do a C gracenote while still on Low G.
5) Play a C.

High A – Bubly – D

1) Play High A.
2) Play a Low G.
3) Do a D gracenote while on Low G.
4) Do a C gracenote while still on Low G.
5) Play a D.

High A – Bubly – E

1) Play High A.
2) Play a Low G.
3) Do a D gracenote while on Low G.
4) Do a C gracenote while still on Low G.
5) Play an E.

High A – Bubly – F

1) Play High A.
2) Play a Low G.
3) Do a D gracenote while on Low G.
4) Do a C gracenote while still on Low G.
5) Play an F.

High A – Bubly – High G

1) Play High A.
2) Play a Low G.
3) Do a D gracenote while on Low G.
4) Do a C gracenote while still on Low G.
5) Play High G.

High A – Bubly – High A

1) Play High A.
2) Play a Low G.
3) Do a D gracenote while on Low G.
4) Do a C gracenote while still on Low G.
5) Play High A.

The Bubly can be played in between any note from Low A to High A and it always ends on a note in between Low A and High A.

Half Bubly

Low G – Half Bubly – Low A

    1) Play Low G.
    2) Do a D gracenote while on Low G.
    3) Do a C gracenote while still on Low G.
    4) Play Low A.

Low G – Half Bubly – B

    1) Play Low G.
    2) Do a D gracenote while on Low G.
    3) Do a C gracenote while still on Low G.
    4) Play a B.

Low G – Half Bubly – C

    1) Play Low G.
    2) Do a D gracenote while on Low G.
    3) Do a C gracenote while still on Low G.
    4) Play a C.

Low G – Half Bubly – D

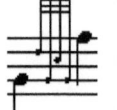
1) Play Low G.
2) Do a D gracenote while on Low G.
3) Do a C gracenote while still on Low G.
4) Play a D.

Low G – Half Bubly – E

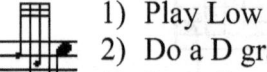
1) Play Low G.
2) Do a D gracenote while on Low G.
3) Do a C gracenote while still on Low G.
4) Play an E.

Low G – Half Bubly – F

1) Play Low G.
2) Do a D gracenote while on Low G.
3) Do a C gracenote while still on Low G.
4) Play an F.

Low G – Half Bubly – High G

1) Play Low G.
2) Do a D gracenote while on Low G.
3) Do a C gracenote while still on Low G.
4) Play High G.

Low G – Half Bubly – High A

1) Play Low G.
2) Do a D gracenote while on Low G.
3) Do a C gracenote while still on Low G.
4) Play High A.

The Half Bubly can only be played from a Low G but it can end on any note in between Low A to High A.

Pele (or Hub-A-Dub)

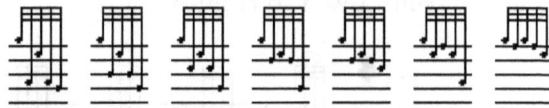

Low A Pele

Low G – Low A Pele

1) Play Low G.
2) Do a G gracenote to Low A.
3) Do an E gracenote while on Low A.
4) Tap your Low A finger to sound a quick Low G then raise it to form a Low A again.

Low A – Low A Pele

1) Play Low A.
2) Do a G gracenote while on Low A.
3) Do an E gracenote while still on Low A.
4) Tap your Low A finger to sound a quick Low G then raise it to form a Low A again.

B – Low A Pele

1) Play a B.
2) Do a G gracenote to Low A.
3) Do an E gracenote while on Low A.
4) Tap your Low A finger to sound a quick Low G then raise it to form a Low A again.

C – Low A Pele

1) Play a C.
2) Do a G gracenote to Low A.
3) Do an E gracenote while on Low A.
4) Tap your Low A finger to sound a quick Low G then raise it to form a Low A again.

D – Low A Pele

1) Play a D.
2) Do a G gracenote to Low A.
3) Do an E gracenote while on Low A.
4) Tap your Low A finger to sound a quick Low G then raise it to form a Low A again.

E – Low A Pele

1) Play an E.
2) Do a G gracenote to Low A.
3) Do an E gracenote while on Low A.
4) Tap your Low A finger to sound a quick Low G then raise it to form a Low A again.

F – Low A Pele

1) Play an F.
2) Do a G gracenote to Low A.
3) Do an E gracenote while on Low A.
4) Tap your Low A finger to sound a quick Low G then raise it to form a Low A again.

The Low A Pele can be played on any note from Low G to F but it always ends on a Low A.

B Pele

Low G – B Pele

1) Play Low G.
2) Do a G gracenote to B.
3) Do an E gracenote while on B.
4) Tap your Low A and B fingers to sound a quick Low G then raise them to form a B again.

Low A – B Pele

1) Play Low A.
2) Do a G gracenote to B.
3) Do an E gracenote while on B.
4) Tap your Low A and B fingers to sound a quick Low G then raise them to form a B again.

B – B Pele

1) Play a B.
2) Do a G gracenote while on B.
3) Do an E gracenote while still on B.
4) Tap your Low A and B fingers to sound a quick Low G then raise them to form a B again.

C – B Pele

1) Play a C.
2) Do a G gracenote to B.
3) Do an E gracenote while on B.
4) Tap your Low A and B fingers to sound a quick Low G then raise them to form a B again.

D – B Pele

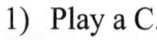
1) Play a D.
2) Do a G gracenote to B.
3) Do an E gracenote while on B.
4) Tap your Low A and B fingers to sound a quick Low G then raise them to form a B again.

E – B Pele

1) Play an E.
2) Do a G gracenote to B.
3) Do an E gracenote while on B.
4) Tap your Low A and B fingers to sound a quick Low G then raise them to form a B again.

F – B Pele

1) Play an F.
2) Do a G gracenote to B.
3) Do an E gracenote while on B.
4) Tap your Low A and B fingers to sound a quick Low G then raise them to form a B again.

The B Pele can be played on any note from Low G to F but it always ends on a B.

C Pele

Low G – C Pele

1) Play Low G.
2) Do a G gracenote to C.
3) Do an E gracenote while on C.
4) Tap your B and C fingers to sound a quick Low G then raise them to form a C again.

Low A – C Pele

1) Play Low A.
2) Do a G gracenote to C.
3) Do an E gracenote while on C.
4) Tap your B and C fingers to sound a quick Low G then raise them to form a C again.

B – C Pele

1) Play a B.
2) Do a G gracenote to C.
3) Do an E gracenote while on C.
4) Tap your B and C fingers to sound a quick Low G then raise them to form a C again.

C – C Pele

1) Play a C.
2) Do a G gracenote while on C.
3) Do an E gracenote while still on C.
4) Tap your B and C fingers to sound a quick Low G then raise them to form a C again.

D – C Pele

1) Play a B.
2) Do a G gracenote to C.
3) Do an E gracenote while on C.
4) Tap your B and C fingers to sound a quick Low G then raise them to form a C again.

E – C Pele

1) Play an E.
2) Do a G gracenote to C.
3) Do an E gracenote while on C.
4) Tap your B and C fingers to sound a quick Low G then raise them to form a C again.

F – C Pele
    1) Play an F.
    2) Do a G gracenote to C.
    3) Do an E gracenote while on C.
    4) Tap your B and C fingers to sound a quick Low G then raise them to form a C again.

The C Pele can be played on any note from Low G to F but it always ends on a C.

D Pele

Low G – D Pele
    1) Play Low G.
    2) Do a G gracenote to D.
    3) Do an E gracenote while on D.
    4) Tap your D, C, and B fingers to sound a quick Low G then raise them to form a D again.

Low A – D Pele
    1) Play Low A.
    2) Do a G gracenote to D.
    3) Do an E gracenote while on D.
    4) Tap your D, C, and B fingers to sound a quick Low G then raise them to form a D again.

B – D Pele

1) Play a B.
2) Do a G gracenote to D.
3) Do an E gracenote while on D.
4) Tap your D, C, and B fingers to sound a quick Low G then raise them to form a D again.

C – D Pele

1) Play a C.
2) Do a G gracenote to D.
3) Do an E gracenote while on D.
4) Tap your D, C, and B fingers to sound a quick Low G then raise them to form a D again.

D – D Pele

1) Play a D.
2) Do a G gracenote while on D.
3) Do an E gracenote while still on D.
4) Tap your D, C, and B fingers to sound a quick Low G then raise them to form a D again.

E – D Pele

1) Play an E.
2) Do a G gracenote to D.
3) Do an E gracenote while on D.
4) Tap your D, C, and B fingers to sound a quick Low G then raise them to form a D again.

F – D Pele

1) Play an F.
2) Do a G gracenote to D.
3) Do an E gracenote while on D.
4) Tap your D, C, and B fingers to sound a quick Low G then raise them to form a D again.

The D Pele can be played on any note from Low G to F but it always ends on a D.

D Pele with a C

Low G – D Pele with a C
1) Play Low G.
2) Do a G gracenote to D.
3) Do an E gracenote while on D.
4) Tap your D finger to sound a quick C then raise it to form a D again.

Low A – D Pele with a C
1) Play Low A.
2) Do a G gracenote to D.
3) Do an E gracenote while on D.
4) Tap your D finger to sound a quick C then raise it to form a D again.

B – D Pele with a C
1) Play a B.
2) Do a G gracenote to D.
3) Do an E gracenote while on D.
4) Tap your D finger to sound a quick C then raise it to form a D again.

C – D Pele with a C

    1) Play a C.
    2) Do a G gracenote to D.
    3) Do an E gracenote while on D.
    4) Tap your D finger to sound a quick C then raise it to form a D again.

D – D Pele with a C

    1) Play a D.
    2) Do a G gracenote while on D.
    3) Do an E gracenote while still on D.
    4) Tap your D finger to sound a quick C then raise it to form a D again.

E – D Pele with a C

    1) Play an E.
    2) Do a G gracenote to D.
    3) Do an E gracenote while on D.
    4) Tap your D finger to sound a quick C then raise it to form a D again.

F – D Pele with a C

    1) Play an F.
    2) Do a G gracenote to D.
    3) Do an E gracenote while on D.
    4) Tap your D finger to sound a quick C then raise it to form a D again.

The D Pele can be played on any note from Low G to F but it always ends on a D.

E Pele

Low G – E Pele

1) Play Low G.
2) Do a G gracenote to E.
3) Do an F gracenote while on E.
4) Tap your E finger to sound a quick Low A then raise it to form an E again.

Low A – E Pele

1) Play Low A.
2) Do a G gracenote to E.
3) Do an F gracenote while on E.
4) Tap your E finger to sound a quick Low A then raise it to form an E again.

B – E Pele

1) Play a B.
2) Do a G gracenote to E.
3) Do an F gracenote while on E.
4) Tap your E finger to sound a quick Low A then raise it to form an E again.

C – E Pele

1) Play a C.
2) Do a G gracenote to E.
3) Do an F gracenote while on E.
4) Tap your E finger to sound a quick Low A then raise it to form an E again.

D – E Pele

1) Play a D.
2) Do a G gracenote to E.
3) Do an F gracenote while on E.
4) Tap your E finger to sound a quick Low A then raise it to form an E again.

E – E Pele

1) Play an E.
2) Do a G gracenote while on E.
3) Do an F gracenote while still on E.
4) Tap your E finger to sound a quick Low A then raise it to form an E again.

F – E Pele

1) Play an F.
2) Do a G gracenote to E.
3) Do an F gracenote while on E.
4) Tap your E finger to sound a quick Low A then raise it to form an E again.

The E Pele can be played on any note from Low G to F but it always ends on an E.

F Pele

Low G – F Pele

1) Play Low G.
2) Do a G gracenote to F.
3) Do another G gracenote while on F.
4) Tap your F finger to sound a quick E then raise it to form an F again.

Low A – F Pele

1) Play Low A.
2) Do a G gracenote to F.
3) Do another G gracenote while on F.
4) Tap your F finger to sound a quick E then raise it to form an F again.

B – F Pele

1) Play a B.
2) Do a G gracenote to F.
3) Do another G gracenote while on F.
4) Tap your F finger to sound a quick E then raise it to form an F again.

C – F Pele

1) Play a C.
2) Do a G gracenote to F.
3) Do another G gracenote while on F.
4) Tap your F finger to sound a quick E then raise it to form an F again.

D – F Pele

1) Play a D.
2) Do a G gracenote to F.
3) Do another G gracenote while on F.
4) Tap your F finger to sound a quick E then raise it to form an F again.

E – F Pele

1) Play an E.
2) Do a G gracenote to F.
3) Do another G gracenote while on F.
4) Tap your F finger to sound a quick E then raise it to form an F again.

F – F Pele

1) Play an F.
2) Do a G gracenote while on F.
3) Do another G gracenote while still on F.
4) Tap your F finger to sound a quick E then raise it to form an F again.

The F Pele can be played on any note from Low G to F but it always ends on an F.

Thumb Pele

Thumb Pele's

Low G – Low A Thumb Pele
1) Play Low G.
2) Play a High A.
3) Play a Low A.
4) Do an E gracenote while on Low A.
5) Tap your Low A finger to sound a quick Low G then raise it to form a Low A again.

Low A – Low A Thumb Pele
1) Play Low A.
2) Play a High A.
3) Play a Low A.
4) Do an E gracenote while on Low A.
5) Tap your Low A finger to sound a quick Low G then raise it to form a Low A again.

B – Low A Thumb Pele
1) Play a B.
2) Play a High A.
3) Play a Low A.
4) Do an E gracenote while on Low A.
5) Tap your Low A finger to sound a quick Low G then raise it to form a Low A again.

C – Low A Thumb Pele
1) Play a C.
2) Play a High A.
3) Play a Low A.
4) Do an E gracenote while on Low A.
5) Tap your Low A finger to sound a quick Low G then raise it to form a Low A again.

D – Low A Thumb Pele
1) Play a D.
2) Play a High A.
3) Play a Low A.
4) Do an E gracenote while on Low A.
5) Tap your Low A finger to sound a quick Low G then raise it to form a Low A again.

E – Low A Thumb Pele

1) Play an E.
2) Play a High A.
3) Play a Low A.
4) Do an E gracenote while on Low A.
5) Tap your Low A finger to sound a quick Low G then raise it to form a Low A again.

F – Low A Thumb Pele
1) Play an F.
2) Play a High A.
3) Play a Low A.
4) Do an E gracenote while on Low A.
5) Tap your Low A finger to sound a quick Low G then raise it to form a Low A again.

High G – Low A Thumb Pele
  1) Play High G.
  2) Play a High A.
  3) Play a Low A.
  4) Do an E gracenote while on Low A.
  5) Tap your Low A finger to sound a quick Low G then raise it to form a Low A again.

The Low A Thumb Pele can be played on any note from Low G to High G but it always ends on a Low A.

B Thumb Pele

Low G – B Thumb Pele
  1) Play Low G.
  2) Play a High A.
  3) Play a B.
  4) Do an E gracenote while on B.
  5) Tap your Low A and B finger to sound a quick Low G then raise them to form a B again.

Low A – B Thumb Pele
1) Play Low A.
2) Play a High A.
3) Play a B.
4) Do an E gracenote while on B.
5) Tap your Low A and B finger to sound a quick Low G then raise them to form a B again.

B – B Thumb Pele
1) Play a B.
2) Play a High A.
3) Play a B again.
4) Do an E gracenote while still on B.
5) Tap your Low A and B finger to sound a quick Low G then raise them to form a B again.

C – B Thumb Pele
1) Play a C.
2) Play a High A.
3) Play a B.
4) Do an E gracenote while on B.
5) Tap your Low A and B finger to sound a quick Low G then raise them to form a B again.

D – B Thumb Pele
1) Play a D.
2) Play a High A.
3) Play a B.
4) Do an E gracenote while on B.
5) Tap your Low A and B finger to sound a quick Low G then raise them to form a B again.

E – B Thumb Pele

1) Play an E.
2) Play a High A.
3) Play a B.
4) Do an E gracenote while on B.
5) Tap your Low A and B finger to sound a quick Low G then raise them to form a B again.

F – B Thumb Pele

1) Play an F.
2) Play a High A.
3) Play a B.
4) Do an E gracenote while on B.
5) Tap your Low A and B finger to sound a quick Low G then raise them to form a B again.

High G – B Thumb Pele

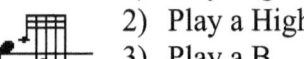

1) Play High G.
2) Play a High A.
3) Play a B.
4) Do an E gracenote while on B.
5) Tap your Low A and B finger to sound a quick Low G then raise them to form a B again.

The B Thumb Pele can be played on any note from Low G to High G but it always ends on a B.

C Thumb Pele

Low G – C Thumb Pele
1) Play Low G.
2) Play a High A.
3) Play a C.
4) Do an E gracenote while on C.
5) Tap your B and C finger to sound a quick Low G then raise them to form a C again.

Low A – C Thumb Pele
1) Play Low A.
2) Play a High A.
3) Play a C.
4) Do an E gracenote while on C.
5) Tap your B and C finger to sound a quick Low G then raise them to form a C again.

B – C Thumb Pele
1) Play a B.
2) Play a High A.
3) Play a C.
4) Do an E gracenote while on C.
5) Tap your B and C finger to sound a quick Low G then raise them to form a C again.

C – C Thumb Pele
1) Play a C.
2) Play a High A.
3) Play a C again.
4) Do an E gracenote while on C.
5) Tap your B and C finger to sound a quick Low G then raise them to form a C again.

D – C Thumb Pele

1) Play a D.
2) Play a High A.
3) Play a C.
4) Do an E gracenote while on C.
5) Tap your B and C finger to sound a quick Low G then raise them to form a C again.

E – C Thumb Pele

1) Play an E.
2) Play a High A.
3) Play a C.
4) Do an E gracenote while on C.
5) Tap your B and C finger to sound a quick Low G then raise them to form a C again.

F – C Thumb Pele

1) Play an F.
2) Play a High A.
3) Play a C.
4) Do an E gracenote while on C.
5) Tap your B and C finger to sound a quick Low G then raise them to form a C again.

High G – C Thumb Pele

1) Play High G.
2) Play a High A.
3) Play a C.
4) Do an E gracenote while on C.
5) Tap your B and C finger to sound a quick Low G then raise them to form a C again.

The C Thumb Pele can be played on any note from Low G to High G but it always ends on a C.

D Thumb Pele

Low G – D Thumb Pele

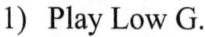
1) Play Low G.
2) Play a High A.
3) Play a D.
4) Do an E gracenote while on D.
5) Tap your B, C and D fingers to sound a quick Low G then raise them to form a D again.

Low A – D Thumb Pele

1) Play Low A.
2) Play a High A.
3) Play a D.
4) Do an E gracenote while on D.
5) Tap your B, C and D fingers to sound a quick Low G then raise them to form a D again.

B – D Thumb Pele

1) Play a B.
2) Play a High A.
3) Play a D.
4) Do an E gracenote while on D.
5) Tap your B, C and D fingers to sound a quick Low G then raise them to form a D again.

C – D Thumb Pele

1) Play a C.
2) Play a High A.
3) Play a D.
4) Do an E gracenote while on D.
5) Tap your B, C and D fingers to sound a quick Low G then raise them to form a D again.

D – D Thumb Pele

1) Play a D.
2) Play a High A.
3) Play a D again.
4) Do an E gracenote while on D.
5) Tap your B, C and D fingers to sound a quick Low G then raise them to form a D again.

E – D Thumb Pele

1) Play an E.
2) Play a High A.
3) Play a D.
4) Do an E gracenote while on D.
5) Tap your B, C and D fingers to sound a quick Low G then raise them to form a D again.

F – D Thumb Pele

1) Play an F.
2) Play a High A.
3) Play a D.
4) Do an E gracenote while on D.
5) Tap your B, C and D fingers to sound a quick Low G then raise them to form a D again.

High G – D Thumb Pele
1) Play High G.
2) Play a High A.
3) Play a D.
4) Do an E gracenote while on D.
5) Tap your B, C and D fingers to sound a quick Low G then raise them to form a D again.

The D Thumb Pele can be played on any note from Low G to High G but it always ends on a D.

D Thumb Pele with a C

Low G – D Thumb Pele with a C
1) Play Low G.
2) Play a High A.
3) Play a D.
4) Do an E gracenote while on D.
5) Tap your D finger to sound a quick C then raise it to form a D again.

Low A – D Thumb Pele with a C
1) Play Low A.
2) Play a High A.
3) Play a D.
4) Do an E gracenote while on D.
5) Tap your D finger to sound a quick C then raise it to form a D again.

B – D Thumb Pele with a C
1) Play a B.
2) Play a High A.
3) Play a D.
4) Do an E gracenote while on D.
5) Tap your D finger to sound a quick C then raise it to form a D again.

C – D Thumb Pele with a C
1) Play a C.
2) Play a High A.
3) Play a D.
4) Do an E gracenote while on D.
5) Tap your D finger to sound a quick C then raise it to form a D again.

D – D Thumb Pele with a C
1) Play a D.
2) Play a High A.
3) Play a D again.
4) Do an E gracenote while on D.
5) Tap your D finger to sound a quick C then raise it to form a D again.

E – D Thumb Pele with a C
1) Play an E.
2) Play a High A.
3) Play a D.
4) Do an E gracenote while on D.
5) Tap your D finger to sound a quick C then raise it to form a D again.

F – D Thumb Pele with a C
1) Play an F.
2) Play a High A.
3) Play a D.
4) Do an E gracenote while on D.
5) Tap your D finger to sound a quick C then raise it to form a D again.

High G – D Thumb Pele with a C
1) Play High G.
2) Play a High A.
3) Play a D.
4) Do an E gracenote while on D.
5) Tap your D finger to sound a quick C then raise it to form a D again.

The D Thumb Pele can be played on any note from Low G to High G but it always ends on a D.

E Thumb Pele

Low G – E Thumb Pele

1) Play Low G.
2) Play a High A.
3) Play an E.
4) Do an F gracenote while on E.
5) Tap your E finger to sound a quick Low A then raise it to form an E again.

Low A – E Thumb Pele

1) Play Low A.
2) Play a High A.
3) Play an E.
4) Do an F gracenote while on E.
5) Tap your E finger to sound a quick Low A then raise it to form an E again.

B – E Thumb Pele

1) Play a B.
2) Play a High A.
3) Play an E.
4) Do an F gracenote while on E.
5) Tap your E finger to sound a quick Low A then raise it to form an E again.

C – E Thumb Pele

1) Play a C.
2) Play a High A.
3) Play an E.
4) Do an F gracenote while on E.
5) Tap your E finger to sound a quick Low A then raise it to form an E again.

D – E Thumb Pele
1) Play a D.
2) Play a High A.
3) Play an E.
4) Do an F gracenote while on E.
5) Tap your E finger to sound a quick Low A then raise it to form an E again.

E – E Thumb Pele
1) Play an E.
2) Play a High A.
3) Play an E again.
4) Do an F gracenote while on E.
5) Tap your E finger to sound a quick Low A then raise it to form an E again.

F – E Thumb Pele
1) Play an F.
2) Play a High A.
3) Play an E.
4) Do an F gracenote while on E.
5) Tap your E finger to sound a quick Low A then raise it to form an E again.

High G – E Thumb Pele
1) Play High G.
2) Play a High A.
3) Play an E.
4) Do an F gracenote while on E.
5) Tap your E finger to sound a quick Low A then raise it to form an E again.

The E Thumb Pele can be played on any note from Low G to High G but it always ends on an E.

F Thumb Pele

Low G – F Thumb Pele
1) Play Low G.
2) Play a High A.
3) Play an F.
4) Do a G gracenote while on F.
5) Tap your F finger to sound a quick E then raise it to form an F again.

Low A – F Thumb Pele
1) Play Low A.
2) Play a High A.
3) Play an F.
4) Do a G gracenote while on F.
5) Tap your F finger to sound a quick E then raise it to form an F again.

B – F Thumb Pele
1) Play a B.
2) Play a High A.
3) Play an F.
4) Do a G gracenote while on F.
5) Tap your F finger to sound a quick E then raise it to form an F again.

C – F Thumb Pele

1) Play a C.
2) Play a High A.
3) Play an F.
4) Do a G gracenote while on F.
5) Tap your F finger to sound a quick E then raise it to form an F again.

D – F Thumb Pele

1) Play a D.
2) Play a High A.
3) Play an F.
4) Do a G gracenote while on F.
5) Tap your F finger to sound a quick E then raise it to form an F again.

E – F Thumb Pele

1) Play an E.
2) Play a High A.
3) Play an F.
4) Do a G gracenote while on F.
5) Tap your F finger to sound a quick E then raise it to form an F again.

F – F Thumb Pele

1) Play an F.
2) Play a High A.
3) Play an F.
4) Do a G gracenote while on F.
5) Tap your F finger to sound a quick E then raise it to form an F again.

High G – F Thumb Pele

    1) Play High G.
    2) Play a High A.
    3) Play an F.
    4) Do a G gracenote while on F.
    5) Tap your F finger to sound a quick E then raise it to form an F again.

The F Thumb Pele can be played on any note from Low G to High G but it always ends on an F.

High G Thumb Pele

Low G – High G Thumb Pele

    1) Play Low G.
    2) Play a High A.
    3) Play a High G.
    4) Play High A again.
    5) Play Low G again.
    6) Tap your High G finger to sound a quick F then raise it to form a High G again.

Low A – High G Thumb Pele
1) Play Low A.
2) Play a High A.
3) Play a High G.
4) Play High A again.
5) Play High G again.
6) Tap your High G finger to sound a quick F then raise it to form a High G again.

B – High G Thumb Pele
1) Play a B.
2) Play a High A.
3) Play a High G.
4) Play High A again.
5) Play High G again.
6) Tap your High G finger to sound a quick F then raise it to form a High G again.

C – High G Thumb Pele
1) Play a C.
2) Play a High A.
3) Play a High G.
4) Play High A again.
5) Play High G again.
6) Tap your High G finger to sound a quick F then raise it to form a High G again.

D – High G Thumb Pele
1) Play a D.
2) Play a High A.
3) Play a High G.
4) Play High A again.
5) Play High G again.
6) Tap your High G finger to sound a quick F then raise it to form a High G again.

E – High G Thumb Pele

1) Play an E.
2) Play a High A.
3) Play a High G.
4) Play High A again.
5) Play High G again.
6) Tap your High G finger to sound a quick F then raise it to form a High G again.

F – High G Thumb Pele

1) Play an F.
2) Play a High A.
3) Play a High G.
4) Play High A again.
5) Play High G again.
6) Tap your High G finger to sound a quick F then raise it to form a High G again.

High G – High G Thumb Pele

1) Play a High G.
2) Play a High A.
3) Play High G again.
4) Play High A again.
5) Play another High G.
6) Tap your High G finger to sound a quick F then raise it to form a High G.

The High G Thumb Pele can be played on any note from Low G to High G but it always ends on a High G.

Half Pele

Half Pele

Low A Half Pele

1) Play High A.
2) Play a Low A.
3) Do an E gracenote while on Low A.
4) Tap your Low A finger to sound a quick Low G then raise it to form a Low A again.

The Low A Half Pele is usually played from a High A but it always ends on a Low A.

B Half Pele

1) Play High A.
2) Play a B.
3) Do an E gracenote while on B.
4) Tap your Low A and B fingers to sound a quick Low G then raise it to form a B again.

The B Half Pele is usually played from a High A but it always ends on a B.

C Half Pele

1) Play High A.
2) Play a C.
3) Do an E gracenote while on C.
4) Tap your B and C fingers to sound a quick Low G then raise it to form a C again.

The C Half Pele is usually played from a High A but it always ends on a C.

D Half Pele

1) Play High A.
2) Play a D.
3) Do an E gracenote while on D.
4) Tap your D, C and B fingers to sound a quick Low G then raise them to form a D again.

The D Half Pele is usually played from a High A but it always ends on a D.

D Half Pele with a C

1) Play High A.
2) Play a D.
3) Do an E gracenote while on D.
4) Tap your D finger to sound a quick Low C them raise it to form a C again.

The D Half Pele is usually played from a High A but it always ends on a D.

231

E Half Pele

1) Play High A.
2) Play an E.
3) Do an F gracenote while on D.
4) Tap your E finger to sound a quick Low A then raise it to form an E again.

The E Half Pele is usually played from a High A but it always ends on an E.

F Half Pele

1) Play High A.
2) Play an F.
3) Do a G gracenote while on F.
4) Tap your F gracenote to sound a quick E then raise it to form an F again.

The F Half Pele is usually played from a High A but it always ends on an F.

High G Half Pele

1) Play a High A.
2) Play a High G.
3) Play High A again.
4) Play High G again.
5) Tap your High G finger to sound a quick F then raise it to form an F again.

The High G Half Pele is usually played from a High A but it always ends on High G.

Double Strikes

Double Strikes

Low A Double Strike

1) Play Low A.
2) Tap your Low A finger twice to sound two quick Low G's finishing on a Low A.

B Double Strike

1) Play a B.
2) Tap your Low A and B fingers twice to sound two quick Low G's finishing on a B.

C Double Strike

1) Play a C.
2) Tap your B and C fingers twice to sound two quick Low G's finishing on a C.

D Double Strike

1) Play a D.
2) Tap your B, C, and D fingers twice to sound two quick Low G's finishing on a D.

D Double Strike with a C

1) Play a D.
2) Tap your D finger twice to sound two quick C's finishing on a D.

E Double Strike

1) Play an E.
2) Tap your E finger twice to sound two quick Low A's finishing on an E.

F Double Strike

1) Play an F.
2) Tap your F finger twice to sound two quick E's finishing on an F.

High G Double Strike

1) Play High G.
2) Tap your High G finger twice to sound two quick F's finishing on a High G.

High A Double Strike

1) Play High A.
2) Tap your High A finger twice to sound two quick High G's finishing on a High A.

G Double Strikes

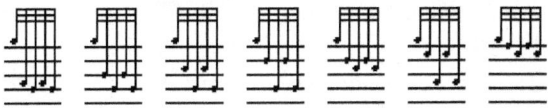

G Double Strikes to Low A

Low G – G Double Strike on Low A

1) Play Low G.
2) Do a G gracenote to Low A.
3) Tap your Low A finger twice to sound two quick Low G's finishing on a Low A.

Low A – G Double Strike on Low A

1) Play Low A.
2) Do a G gracenote while on Low A.
3) Tap your Low A finger twice to sound two quick Low G's finishing on a Low A.

B – G Double Strike on Low A

1) Play a B.
2) Do a G gracenote to Low A.
3) Tap your Low A finger twice to sound two quick Low G's finishing on a Low A.

C – G Double Strike on Low A

1) Play a C.
2) Do a G gracenote to Low A.
3) Tap your Low A finger twice to sound two quick Low G's finishing on a Low A.

D – G Double Strike on Low A

1) Play a D.
2) Do a G gracenote to Low A.
3) Tap your Low A finger twice to sound two quick Low G's finishing on a Low A.

E – G Double Strike on Low A

1) Play an E.
2) Do a G gracenote to Low A.
3) Tap your Low A finger twice to sound two quick Low G's finishing on a Low A.

F – G Double Strike on Low A

1) Play an F.
2) Do a G gracenote to Low A.
3) Tap your Low A finger twice to sound two quick Low G's finishing on a Low A.

The G Double Strike can be played on any note from Low A to F but it always ends on a Low A. The G Double Strike also looks just like the 'G Birl' and it can be played like it to, they are interchangeable.

G Double Strike to B

Low G – G Double Strike on B

1) Play Low G.
2) Do a G gracenote to B.
3) Tap your Low A and B fingers to sound two quick Low G's finishing on a B.

Low A – G Double Strike on B

1) Play Low A.
2) Do a G gracenote to B.
3) Tap your Low A and B fingers to sound two quick Low G's finishing on a B.

B – G Double Strike on B

1) Play a B.
2) Do a G gracenote while still on B.
3) Tap your Low A and B fingers to sound two quick Low G's finishing on a B.

C – G Double Strike on B

1) Play a C.
2) Do a G gracenote to B.
3) Tap your Low A and B fingers to sound two quick Low G's finishing on a B.

D – G Double Strike on B

1) Play a D.
2) Do a G gracenote to B.
3) Tap your Low A and B fingers to sound two quick Low G's finishing on a B.

E – G Double Strike on B

1) Play an E.
2) Do a G gracenote to B.
3) Tap your Low A and B fingers to sound two quick Low G's finishing on a B.

F – G Double Strike on B

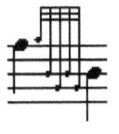
1) Play an F.
2) Do a G gracenote to B.
3) Tap your Low A and B fingers to sound two quick Low G's finishing on a B.

The G Double Strike on B can be played on any note from Low G to F but it always ends on a B.

G Double Strike on C

Low G – G Double Strike on C

1) Play Low G.
2) Do a G gracenote to C.
3) Tap your B and C fingers to sound two quick Low G's finishing on a C.

Low A – G Double Strike on C

1) Play Low A.
2) Do a G gracenote to C.
3) Tap your B and C fingers to sound two quick Low G's finishing on a C.

B – G Double Strike on C

1) Play a B.
2) Do a G gracenote to C.
3) Tap your B and C fingers to sound two quick Low G's finishing on a C.

C – G Double Strike on C

1) Play a C.
2) Do a G gracenote while still on C.
3) Tap your B and C fingers to sound two quick Low G's finishing on a C.

D – G Double Strike on C

1) Play a D.
2) Do a G gracenote to C.
3) Tap your B and C fingers to sound two quick Low G's finishing on a C.

E – G Double Strike on C

1) Play an E.
2) Do a G gracenote to C.
3) Tap your B and C fingers to sound two quick Low G's finishing on a C.

F – G Double Strike on C

1) Play an F.
2) Do a G gracenote to C.
3) Tap your B and C fingers to sound two quick Low G's finishing on a C.

The G Double Strike on C can be played on any note from Low G to F but it always ends on a C.

G Double Strike on D

Low G – G Double Strike on D

1) Play Low G.
2) Do a G gracenote to D.
3) Tap your B, C, and D fingers to sound two quick Low G's finishing on a D.

Low A – G Double Strike on D

1) Play Low A.
2) Do a G gracenote to D.
3) Tap your B, C, and D fingers to sound two quick Low G' finishing on a D.

B – G Double Strike on D

1) Play a B.
2) Do a G gracenote to D.
3) Tap your B, C, and D fingers to sound two quick Low G's finishing on a D.

C – G Double Strike on D

1) Play a C.
2) Do a G gracenote to D.
3) Tap your B, C, and D fingers to sound two quick Low G's finishing on a D.

D – G Double Strike on D

1) Play a D.
2) Do a G gracenote while still on D.
3) Tap your B, C, and D fingers to sound two quick Low G's finishing on a D.

E – G Double Strike on D

1) Play an E.
2) Do a G gracenote to D.
3) Tap your B, C, and D fingers to sound two quick Low G's finishing on a D.

F – G Double Strike on D

1) Play an F.
2) Do a G gracenote to D.
3) Tap your B, C, and D fingers to sound two quick Low G's finishing on a D.

The G Double Strike on D can be played on any note from Low G to F but it always ends on a D.

G Double Strike on D with a C

Low G – G Double Strike on D with a C

    1) Play Low G.
    2) Do a G gracenote to D.
    3) Tap your D finger twice to sound two quick C's finishing on a D.

Low A – G Double Strike on D with a C

    1) Play Low A.
    2) Do a G gracenote to D.
    3) Tap your D finger twice to sound two quick C's finishing on a D.

B – G Double Strike on D with a C

    1) Play a B.
    2) Do a G gracenote to D.
    3) Tap your D finger twice to sound two quick C's finishing on a D.

C – G Double Strike on D with a C

    1) Play a C.
    2) Do a G gracenote to D.
    3) Tap your D finger twice to sound two quick C's finishing on a D.

D – G Double Strike on D with a C

1) Play a D.
2) Do a G gracenote while still on D.
3) Tap your D finger twice to sound two quick C's finishing on a D.

E – G Double Strike on D with a C

1) Play an E.
2) Do a G gracenote to D.
3) Tap your D finger twice to sound two quick C's finishing on a D.

F – G Double Strike on D with a C

1) Play an F.
2) Do a G gracenote to D.
3) Tap your D finger twice to sound two quick C's finishing on a D.

The G Double Strike on D with a C can be played on any note from Low G to F but it always ends on a D.

G Double Strike on E

Low G – G Double Strike on E

1) Play Low G.
2) Do a G gracenote to E.
3) Tap your E finger twice to sound two quick Low A's finishing on an E.

Low A – G Double Strike on E

    1) Play Low A.
    2) Do a G gracenote to E.
    3) Tap your E finger twice to sound two quick Low A's finishing on an E.

B – G Double Strike on E

    1) Play a B.
    2) Do a G gracenote to E.
    3) Tap your E finger twice to sound two quick Low A's finishing on an E.

C – G Double Strike on E

    1) Play a C.
    2) Do a G gracenote to E.
    3) Tap your E finger twice to sound two quick Low A's finishing on an E.

D – G Double Strike on E

    1) Play a D.
    2) Do a G gracenote to E.
    3) Tap your E finger twice to sound two quick Low A's finishing on an E.

E – G Double Strike on E

    1) Play an E.
    2) Do a G gracenote while still on E.
    3) Tap your E finger twice to sound two quick Low A's finishing on an E.

F – G Double Strike on E

    1) Play an F.
    2) Do a G gracenote to E.
    3) Tap your E finger twice to sound two quick Low A's finishing on an E.

The G Double Strike on B can be played on any note from Low G to F but it always ends on a B.

G Double Strike on F

Low G – G Double Strike on F

1) Play Low G.
2) Do a G gracenote to F.
3) Tap your F finger twice to sound two quick E's finishing on an F.

Low A – G Double Strike on F

1) Play Low A.
2) Do a G gracenote to F.
3) Tap your F finger twice to sound two quick E's finishing on an F.

B – G Double Strike on F

1) Play a B.
2) Do a G gracenote to F.
3) Tap your F finger twice to sound two quick E's finishing on an F.

C – G Double Strike on F

1) Play a C.
2) Do a G gracenote to F.
3) Tap your F finger twice to sound two quick E's finishing on an F.

D – G Double Strike on F

1) Play a D.
2) Do a G gracenote to F.
3) Tap your F finger twice to sound two quick E's finishing on an F.

E – G Double Strike on F

1) Play an E.
2) Do a G gracenote to F.
3) Tap your F finger twice to sound two quick E's finishing on an F.

F – G Double Strike on F

1) Play an F.
2) Do a G gracenote while still on F.
3) Tap your F finger twice to sound two quick E's finishing on an F.

The G Double Strike on F can be played on any note from Low G to F but it always ends on a F.

Thumb Double Strikes

Thumb Double Strike on Low A

Low G – Thumb Double Strike on Low A

1) Play Low G.
2) Play High A.
3) Play Low A.
4) Tap your Low A finger twice to sound two quick Low G's finishing on a Low A.

Low A – Thumb Double Strike on Low A

1) Play Low A.
2) Play High A.
3) Play Low A again.
4) Tap your Low A finger twice to sound two quick Low G's finishing on a Low A.

B – Thumb Double Strike on Low A

1) Play a B.
2) Play High A.
3) Play Low A.
4) Tap your Low A finger twice to sound two quick Low G's finishing on a Low A.

C – Thumb Double Strike on Low A

1) Play a C.
2) Play High A.
3) Play Low A.
4) Tap your Low A finger twice to sound two quick Low G's finishing on a Low A.

D – Thumb Double Strike on Low A

1) Play a D.
2) Play High A.
3) Play Low A.
4) Tap your Low A finger twice to sound two quick Low G's finishing on a Low A.

E – Thumb Double Strike on Low A

1) Play an E.
2) Play High A.
3) Play Low A.
4) Tap your Low A finger twice to sound two quick Low G's finishing on a Low A.

F – Thumb Double Strike on Low A

1) Play an F.
2) Play High A.
3) Play Low A.
4) Tap your Low A finger twice to sound two quick Low G's finishing on a Low A.

High G – Thumb Double Strike on Low A

1) Play High G.
2) Play High A.
3) Play Low A.
4) Tap your Low A finger twice to sound two quick Low G's finishing on a Low A.

The Thumb Double Strike on Low A can be played on any note from Low G to High G but it always ends on Low A.

Thumb Double Strike on B

Low G – Thumb Double Strike on B

1) Play Low G.
2) Play High A.
3) Play a B.
4) Tap your Low A and B fingers twice to sound two quick Low G's finishing on a B.

Low A – Thumb Double Strike on B

1) Play Low A.
2) Play High A.
3) Play a B.
4) Tap your Low A and B fingers twice to sound two quick Low G's finishing on a B.

B – Thumb Double Strike on B

1) Play a B.
2) Play High A.
3) Play a B again.
4) Tap your Low A and B fingers twice to sound two quick Low G's finishing on a B.

C – Thumb Double Strike on B

1) Play a C.
2) Play High A.
3) Play a B.
4) Tap your Low A and B fingers twice to sound two quick Low G's finishing on a B.

D – Thumb Double Strike on B

1) Play a D.
2) Play High A.
3) Play a B.
4) Tap your Low A and B fingers twice to sound two quick Low G's finishing on a B.

E – Thumb Double Strike on B

1) Play an E.
2) Play High A.
3) Play a B.
4) Tap your Low A and B fingers twice to sound two quick Low G's finishing on a B.

F – Thumb Double Strike on B

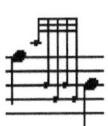
1) Play an F.
2) Play High A.
3) Play a B.
4) Tap your Low A and B fingers twice to sound two quick Low G's finishing on a B.

High G – Thumb Double Strike on B

1) Play High G.
2) Play High A.
3) Play a B.
4) Tap your Low A and B fingers twice to sound two quick Low G's finishing on a B.

The Thumb Double Strike on B can be played on any note from Low G to High G but it always ends on a B.

Thumb Double Strike on C

Low G – Thumb Double Strike on C
1) Play Low G.
2) Play High A.
3) Play a C.
4) Tap your B and C fingers twice to sound two quick Low G's finishing on a C.

Low A – Thumb Double Strike on C
1) Play Low A.
2) Play High A.
3) Play a C.
4) Tap your B and C fingers twice to sound two quick Low G's finishing on a C.

B – Thumb Double Strike on C
1) Play a B.
2) Play High A.
3) Play a C.
4) Tap your B and C fingers twice to sound two quick Low G's finishing on a C.

C – Thumb Double Strike on C
1) Play a C.
2) Play High A.
3) Play a C again.
4) Tap your B and C fingers twice to sound two quick Low G's finishing on a C.

D – Thumb Double Strike on C
1) Play a D.
2) Play High A.
3) Play a C.
4) Tap your B and C fingers twice to sound two quick Low G's finishing on a C.

E – Thumb Double Strike on C

1) Play an E.
2) Play High A.
3) Play a C.
4) Tap your B and C fingers twice to sound two quick Low G's finishing on a C.

F – Thumb Double Strike on C

1) Play an F.
2) Play High A.
3) Play a C.
4) Tap your B and C fingers twice to sound two quick Low G's finishing on a C.

High G – Thumb Double Strike on C

1) Play High G.
2) Play High A.
3) Play a C.
4) Tap your B and C fingers twice to sound two quick Low G's finishing on a C.

The Thumb Double Strike on C can be played on any note from Low G to High G but it always ends on C.

Thumb Double Strike on D

Low G – Thumb Double Strike on D
1) Play Low G.
2) Play High A.
3) Play a D.
4) Tap your B, C, and D fingers twice to sound two quick Low G's finishing on a D.

Low A – Thumb Double Strike on D

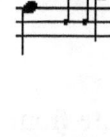

1) Play Low A.
2) Play High A.
3) Play a D.
4) Tap your B, C, and D fingers twice to sound two quick Low G's finishing on a D.

B – Thumb Double Strike on D
1) Play a B.
2) Play High A.
3) Play a D.
4) Tap your B, C, and D fingers twice to sound two quick Low G's finishing on a D.

C – Thumb Double Strike on D
1) Play a C.
2) Play High A.
3) Play a D.
4) Tap your B, C, and D fingers twice to sound two quick Low G's finishing on a D.

D – Thumb Double Strike on D
1) Play a D.
2) Play High A.
3) Play a D again.
4) Tap your B, C, and D fingers twice to sound two quick Low G's finishing on a D.

E – Thumb Double Strike on D

1) Play an E.
2) Play High A.
3) Play a D.
4) Tap your B, C, and D fingers twice to sound two quick Low G's finishing on a D.

F – Thumb Double Strike on D

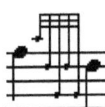
1) Play an F.
2) Play High A.
3) Play a D.
4) Tap your B, C, and D fingers twice to sound two quick Low G's finishing on a D.

High G – Thumb Double Strike on D

1) Play High G.
2) Play High A.
3) Play a D.
4) Tap your B, C, and D fingers twice to sound two quick Low G's finishing on a D.

The Thumb Double Strike on D can be played on any note from Low G to High G but it always ends on a D.

Thumb Double Strike on D with a C

Low G – Thumb Double Strike on D with a C

1) Play Low G.
2) Play High A.
3) Play a D.
4) Tap your C finger twice to sound two quick C's finishing on a D.

Low A – Thumb Double Strike on D with a C

1) Play Low A.
2) Play High A.
3) Play a D.
4) Tap your C finger twice to sound two quick C's finishing on a D.

B – Thumb Double Strike on D with a C

1) Play a B.
2) Play High A.
3) Play a D.
4) Tap your C finger twice to sound two quick C's finishing on a D.

C – Thumb Double Strike on D with a C

1) Play a C.
2) Play High A.
3) Play a D.
4) Tap your C finger twice to sound two quick C's finishing on a D.

D – Thumb Double Strike on D with a C

1) Play a D.
2) Play High A.
3) Play a D again.
4) Tap your C finger twice to sound two quick C's finishing on a D.

E – Thumb Double Strike on D with a C

1) Play an E.
2) Play High A.
3) Play a D.
4) Tap your C finger twice to sound two quick C's finishing on a D.

F – Thumb Doubling Strike on D with a C

1) Play an F.
2) Play High A.
3) Play a D.
4) Tap your C finger twice to sound two quick C's finishing on a D.

High G – Thumb Doubling Strike on D with a C

1) Play High G.
2) Play High A.
3) Play a D.
4) Tap your C finger twice to sound two quick C's finishing on a D.

The Thumb Double Strike on D with a C can be played on any note from Low G to High G but it always ends on a D.

Thumb Doubling Strike on E

Low G – Thumb Doubling Strike on E

1) Play Low G.
2) Play High A.
3) Play an E.
4) Tap your E finger twice to sound two quick Low A's finishing on an E.

Low A – Thumb Double Strike on E

1) Play Low A.
2) Play High A.
3) Play an E.
4) Tap your E finger twice to sound two quick Low A's finishing on an E.

B – Thumb Double Strike on E

1) Play a B.
2) Play High A.
3) Play an E.
4) Tap your E finger twice to sound two quick Low A's finishing on an E.

C – Thumb Double Strike on E

1) Play a C.
2) Play High A.
3) Play an E.
4) Tap your E finger twice to sound two quick Low A's finishing on an E.

D – Thumb Double Strike on E

1) Play a D.
2) Play High A.
3) Play an E.
4) Tap your E finger twice to sound two quick Low A's finishing on an E.

E – Thumb Double Strike on E

1) Play an E.
2) Play High A.
3) Play an E again.
4) Tap your E finger twice to sound two quick Low A's finishing on an E.

F – Thumb Double Strike on E

1) Play an F.
2) Play High A.
3) Play an E.
4) Tap your E finger twice to sound two quick Low A's finishing on an E.

High G – Thumb Double Strike on E

1) Play High G.
2) Play High A.
3) Play an E.
4) Tap your E finger twice to sound two quick Low A's finishing on an E.

The Thumb Double Strike on E with a C can be played on any note from Low G to High G but it always ends on an E.

Thumb Double Strike on F

Low G – Thumb Double Strike on F

1) Play Low G.
2) Play High A.
3) Play an F.
4) Tap your F finger twice to sound two quick E's finishing on an F.

Low A – Thumb Double Strike on F

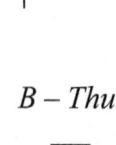

1) Play Low A.
2) Play High A.
3) Play an F.
4) Tap your F finger twice to sound two quick E's finishing on an F.

B – Thumb Double Strike on F

1) Play a B.
2) Play High A.
3) Play an F.
4) Tap your F finger twice to sound two quick E's finishing on an F.

C – Thumb Double Strike on F

1) Play a C.
2) Play High A.
3) Play an F.
4) Tap your F finger twice to sound two quick E's finishing on an F.

D – Thumb Double Strike on F

1) Play a D.
2) Play High A.
3) Play an F.
4) Tap your F finger twice to sound two quick E's finishing on an F.

E – Thumb Double Strike on F

1) Play an E.
2) Play High A.
3) Play an F.
4) Tap your F finger twice to sound two quick E's finishing on an F.

F – Thumb Double Strike on F

1) Play an F.
2) Play High A.
3) Play an F again.
4) Tap your F finger twice to sound two quick E's finishing on an F.

High G – Thumb Double Strike on F

1) Play High G.
2) Play High A.
3) Play an F.
4) Tap your F finger twice to sound two quick E's finishing on an F.

The Thumb Double Strike on F with can be played on any note from Low G to High G but it always ends on an F.

Thumb Double Strike on High G

Low G – Thumb Double Strike on High G
1) Play Low G.
2) Play High A.
3) Play High G.
4) Tap your High G finger twice to make two quick F's finishing on High G.

Low A – Thumb Double Strike on High G
1) Play Low A.
2) Play High A.
3) Play High G.
4) Tap your High G finger twice to make two quick F's finishing on High G.

B – Thumb Double Strike on High G
1) Play a B.
2) Play High A.
3) Play High G.
4) Tap your High G finger twice to make two quick F's finishing on High G.

C – Thumb Double Strike on High G
1) Play a C.
2) Play High A.
3) Play High G.
4) Tap your High G finger twice to make two quick F's finishing on High G.

D – Thumb Double Strike on High G
1) Play a D.
2) Play High A.
3) Play High G.
4) Tap your High G finger twice to make two quick F's finishing on High G.

E – Thumb Double Strike on High G

1) Play an E.
2) Play High A.
3) Play High G.
4) Tap your High G finger twice to make two quick F's finishing on High G.

F – Thumb Double Strike on High G

1) Play an F.
2) Play High A.
3) Play High G.
4) Tap your High G finger twice to make two quick F's finishing on High G.

High G – Thumb Double Strike on High G

1) Play High G.
2) Play High A.
3) Play High G again.
4) Tap your High G finger twice to make two quick F's finishing on High G.

The Thumb Double Strike on High G can be played on any note from Low G to High G but it always ends on a High G.

Half Double Strikes

Half Double Strike on Low A

Low G – Half Double Strike on Low A

1) Play Low G.
2) Play Low A.
3) Tap your Low A finger twice to make two quick Low G's finishing on a Low A.

Low A – Half Double Strike on Low A

1) Play Low A.
2) Tap your Low A finger twice to make two quick Low G's finishing on a Low A.

B – Half Double Strike on Low A

1) Play a B.
2) Play Low A.
3) Tap your Low A finger twice to make two quick Low G's finishing on a Low A.

C – Half Double Strike on Low A

1) Play a C.
2) Play Low A.
3) Tap your Low A finger twice to make two quick Low G's finishing on a Low A.

D – Half Double Strike on Low A

1) Play a D.
2) Play Low A.
3) Tap your Low A finger twice to make two quick Low G's finishing on a Low A.

E – Half Double Strike on Low A

1) Play an E.
2) Play Low A.
3) Tap your Low A finger twice to make two quick Low G's finishing on a Low A.

F – Half Double Strike on Low A

1) Play an F.
2) Play Low A.
3) Tap your Low A finger twice to make two quick Low G's finishing on a Low A.

High G – Half Double Strike on Low A

1) Play High G.
2) Play Low A.
3) Tap your Low A finger twice to make two quick Low G's finishing on a Low A.

High A – Half Double Strike on Low A

1) Play High A.
2) Play Low A.
3) Tap your Low A finger twice to make two quick Low G's finishing on a Low A.

The Half Double Strike on Low A can be played on any note from Low G to High A but it always ends on a Low A.

Half Double Strike on B

Low G – Half Double Strike on B

1) Play Low G.
2) Play a B.
3) Tap your Low A and B fingers twice to make two quick Low G's finishing on a B.

Low A – Half Double Strike on B

1) Play Low A.
2) Play a B.
3) Tap your Low A and B fingers twice to make two quick Low G's finishing on a B.

B – Half Double Strike on B

1) Play a B.
2) Tap your Low A and B fingers twice to make two quick Low G's finishing on a B.

C – Half Double Strike on B

1) Play a C.
2) Play a B.
3) Tap your Low A and B fingers twice to make two quick Low G's finishing on a B.

D – Half Double Strike on B

1) Play a D.
2) Play a B.
3) Tap your Low A and B fingers twice to make two quick Low G's finishing on a B.

E – Half Double Strike on B

1) Play an E.
2) Play a B.
3) Tap your Low A and B fingers twice to make two quick Low G's finishing on a B.

F – Half Double Strike on B

1) Play an F.
2) Play a B.
3) Tap your Low A and B fingers twice to make two quick Low G's finishing on a B.

High G – Half Double Strike on B

1) Play High G.
2) Play a B.
3) Tap your Low A and B fingers twice to make two quick Low G's finishing on a B.

High A – Half Double Strike on B

1) Play High A.
2) Play a B.
3) Tap your Low A and B fingers twice to make two quick Low G's finishing on a B.

The Half Double Strike on B can be played on any note from Low G to High A but it always ends on a B.

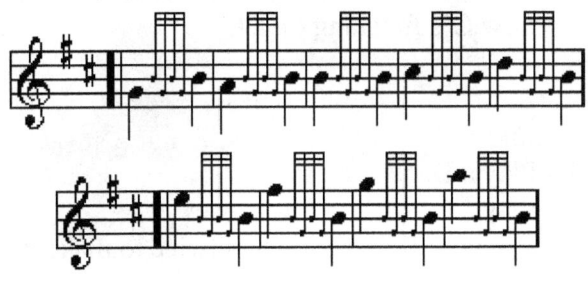

Half Double Strike on C

Low G – Half Double Strike on C

1) Play Low G.
2) Play a C.
3) Tap your B and C fingers twice to make two quick Low G's finishing on a C.

Low A – Half Double Strike on C

1) Play Low A.
2) Play a C.
3) Tap your B and C fingers twice to make two quick Low G's finishing on a C.

B – Half Double Strike on C

1) Play a B.
2) Play a C.
3) Tap your B and C fingers twice to make two quick Low G's finishing on a C.

C – Half Double Strike on C

1) Play a C.
2) Tap your B and C fingers twice to make two quick Low G's finishing on a C.

D – Half Double Strike on C

1) Play a D.
2) Play a C.
3) Tap your B and C fingers twice to make two quick Low G's finishing on a C.

E – Half Double Strike on C

1) Play an E.
2) Play a C.
3) Tap your B and C fingers twice to make two quick Low G's finishing on a C.

F – Half Double Strike on C

1) Play an F.
2) Play a C.
3) Tap your B and C fingers twice to make two quick Low G's finishing on a C.

High G – Half Double Strike on C

1) Play High G.
2) Play a C.
3) Tap your B and C fingers twice to make two quick Low G's finishing on a C.

High A – Half Double Strike on C

1) Play High A.
2) Play a C.
3) Tap your B and C fingers twice to make two quick Low G's finishing on a C.

The Half Double Strike on C can be played on any note from Low G to High A but it always ends on a C.

Half Double Strike on D

Low G – Half Double Strike on D

1) Play Low G.
2) Play a D.
3) Tap your B, C, and D fingers twice to make two quick Low G's finishing on a D.

Low A – Half Double Strike on D

1) Play Low A.
2) Play a D.
3) Tap your B, C, and D fingers twice to make two quick Low G's finishing on a D.

B – Half Double Strike on D

1) Play a B.
2) Play a D.
3) Tap your B, C, and D fingers twice to make two quick Low G's finishing on a D.

C – Half Double Strike on D

1) Play a C.
2) Play a D.
3) Tap your B, C, and D fingers twice to make two quick Low G's finishing on a D.

D – Half Double Strike on D

1) Play a D.
2) Tap your B, C, and D fingers twice to make two quick Low G's finishing on a D.

E – Half Double Strike on D

1) Play an E.
2) Play a D.
3) Tap your B, C, and D fingers twice to make two quick Low G's finishing on a D.

F – Half Double Strike on D

1) Play an F.
2) Play a D.
3) Tap your B, C, and D fingers twice to make two quick Low G's finishing on a D.

High G – Half Double Strike on D

1) Play High G.
2) Play a D.
3) Tap your B, C, and D fingers twice to make two quick Low G's finishing on a D.

High A – Half Double Strike on D

1) Play High A.
2) Play a D.
3) Tap your B, C, and D fingers twice to make two quick Low G's finishing on a D.

The Half Double Strike on D can be played on any note from Low G to High A but it always ends on a D.

Half Double Strike on D with a C

Low G – Half Double Strike on D with a C

1) Play Low G.
2) Play a D.
3) Tap your D finger twice to make two quick C's finishing on a D.

Low A – Half Double Strike on D with a C

1) Play Low A.
2) Play a D.
3) Tap your D finger twice to make two quick C's finishing on a D.

B – Half Double Strike on D with a C

1) Play a B.
2) Play a D.
3) Tap your D finger twice to make two quick C's finishing on a D.

C – Half Double Strike on D with a C

1) Play a C.
2) Play a D.
3) Tap your D finger twice to make two quick C's finishing on a D.

D – Half Double Strike on D with a C

1) Play a D.
2) Tap your D finger twice to make two quick C's finishing on a D.

E – Half Double Strike on D with a C

1) Play an E.
2) Play a D.
3) Tap your D finger twice to make two quick C's finishing on a D.

F – Half Double Strike on D with a C

1) Play an F.
2) Play a D.
3) Tap your D finger twice to make two quick C's finishing on a D.

High G – Half Double Strike on D with a C

1) Play High G.
2) Play a D.
3) Tap your D finger twice to make two quick C's finishing on a D.

High A – Half Double Strike on D with a C

1) Play High A.
2) Play a D.
3) Tap your D finger twice to make two quick C's finishing on a D.

The Half Double Strike on D can be played on any note from Low G to High A but it always ends on a D.

Half Double Strike on E

Low G – Half Double Strike on E

1) Play Low G.
2) Play an E.
3) Tap your E finger twice to make two quick Low A's finishing on an E.

Low A – Half Double Strike on E

1) Play Low A.
2) Play an E.
3) Tap your E finger twice to make two quick Low A's finishing on an E.

B – Half Double Strike on E

1) Play a B.
2) Play an E.
3) Tap your E finger twice to make two quick Low A's finishing on an E.

C – Half Double Strike on E

1) Play a C.
2) Play an E.
3) Tap your E finger twice to make two quick Low A's finishing on an E.

D – Half Double Strike on E

1) Play a D.
2) Play an E.
3) Tap your E finger twice to make two quick Low A's finishing on an E.

E – Half Double Strike on E

1) Play an E.
2) Tap your E finger twice to make two quick Low A's finishing on an E.

F – Half Double Strike on E

1) Play an F.
2) Play an E.
3) Tap your E finger twice to make two quick Low A's finishing on an E.

High G – Half Double Strike on E

1) Play High G.
2) Play an E.
3) Tap your E finger twice to make two quick Low A's finishing on an E.

High A – Half Double Strike on E

1) Play High A.
2) Play an E.
3) Tap your E finger twice to make two quick Low A's finishing on an E.

The Half Double Strike on E can be played on any note from Low G to High A but it always ends on an E.

Half Double Strike on F

Low G – Half Double Strike on F

1) Play Low G.
2) Play an F.
3) Tap your F finger twice to make two quick E's finishing on an F.

Low A – Half Double Strike on F

1) Play Low A.
2) Play an F.
3) Tap your F finger twice to make two quick E's finishing on an F.

B – Half Double Strike on F

1) Play a B.
2) Play an F.
3) Tap your F finger twice to make two quick E's finishing on an F.

C – Half Double Strike on F

1) Play a C.
2) Play an F.
3) Tap your F finger twice to make two quick E's finishing on an F.

D – Half Double Strike on F

1) Play a D.
2) Play an F.
3) Tap your F finger twice to make two quick E's finishing on an F.

E – Half Double Strike on F

1) Play an E.
2) Play an F.
3) Tap your F finger twice to make two quick E's finishing on an F.

F – Half Double Strike on F

    1) Play an F.
    2) Tap your F finger twice to make two quick E's finishing on an F.

High G – Half Double Strike on F

    1) Play High G.
    2) Play an F.
    3) Tap your F finger twice to make two quick E's finishing on an F.

High A – Half Double Strike on F

    1) Play High A.
    2) Play an F.
    3) Tap your F finger twice to make two quick E's finishing on an F.

The Half Double Strike on F can be played on any note from Low G to High A but it always ends on an F.

Half Double Strike on High G

Low G – Half Double Strike on High G

1) Play Low G.
2) Play High G.
3) Tap your High G finger twice to make two quick F's finishing on a High G.

Low A – Half Double Strike on High G

1) Play Low A.
2) Play High G.
3) Tap your High G finger twice to make two quick F's finishing on a High G.

B – Half Double Strike on High G

1) Play a B.
2) Play High G.
3) Tap your High G finger twice to make two quick F's finishing on a High G.

C – Half Double Strike on High G

1) Play a C.
2) Play High G.
3) Tap your High G finger twice to make two quick F's finishing on a High G.

D – Half Double Strike on High G

1) Play a D.
2) Play High G.
3) Tap your High G finger twice to make two quick F's finishing on a High G.

E – Half Double Strike on High G

1) Play an E.
2) Play High G.
3) Tap your High G finger twice to make two quick F's finishing on a High G.

F – Half Double Strike on High G

1) Play an F.
2) Play High G.
3) Tap your High G finger twice to make two quick F's finishing on a High G.

High G – Half Double Strike on High G

1) Play High G.
2) Tap your High G finger twice to make two quick F's finishing on a High G.

High A – Half Double Strike on High G

1) Play High A.
2) Play High G.
3) Tap your High G finger twice to make two quick F's finishing on a High G.

The Half Double Strike on High G can be played on any note from Low G to High A but it always ends on High G.

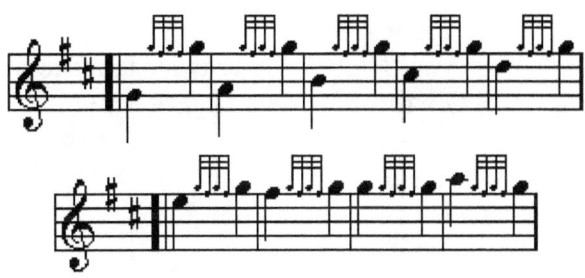

Half Double Strike on High A

Low G – Half Double Strike on High A

1) Play Low G.
2) Play High A.
3) Brush your High A finger twice to make two quick High G's finishing on a High A.

Low A – Half Double Strike on High A

1) Play Low A.
2) Play High A.
3) Brush your High A finger twice to make two quick High G's finishing on a High A.

B – Half Double Strike on High A

1) Play a B.
2) Play High A.
3) Brush your High A finger twice to make two quick High G's finishing on a High A.

C – Half Double Strike on High A

1) Play a C.
2) Play High A.
3) Brush your High A finger twice to make two quick High G's finishing on a High A.

D – Half Double Strike on High A

1) Play a D.
2) Play High A.
3) Brush your High A finger twice to make two quick High G's finishing on a High A.

E – Half Double Strike on High A

1) Play an E.
2) Play High A.
3) Brush your High A finger twice to make two quick High G's finishing on a High A.

F – Half Double Strike on High A

1) Play an F.
2) Play High A.
3) Brush your High A finger twice to make two quick High G's finishing on a High A.

High G – Half Double Strike on High A

1) Play High G.
2) Play High A.
3) Brush your High A finger twice to make two quick High G's finishing on a High A.

High A – Half Double Strike on High A

1) Play High A.
2) Brush your High A finger twice to make two quick High G's finishing on a High A.

The Half Double Strike on High A can be played on any note from Low G to High A but it always ends on High A.

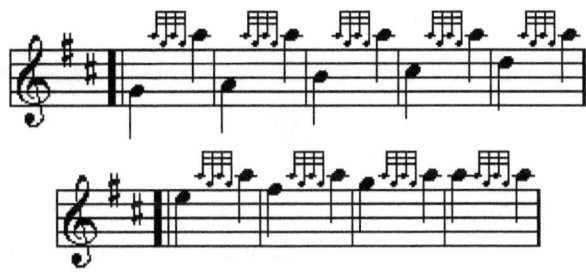

Triple Strike

Triple Strikes

Low A Triple Strike

1) Play Low A.
2) Tap your Low A finger three times to make three quick Low G's finishing on a Low A.

B Triple Strike

1) Play a B.
2) Tap your Low A and B fingers three times to make three quick Low G's finishing on a B.

C Triple Strike

1) Play a C.
2) Tap your B and C fingers three times to make three quick Low G's finishing on a C.

D Triple Strike

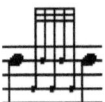
1) Play a D.
2) Tap your B, C, and D fingers three times to make three quick Low G's finishing on a D.

D Triple Strike with a C

1) Play a D.
2) Tap your D finger three times to make three quick C's finishing on a D.

E Triple Strike

1) Play an E.
2) Tap your E finger three times to make three quick Low A's finishing on an E.

F Triple Strike

1) Play an F.
2) Tap your F finger three times to make three quick E's finishing on an F.

High G Triple Strike

1) Play High G.
2) Tap your High G finger three times to make three quick F's finishing on High G.

High A Triple Strike

1) Play High A.
2) Brush your High A finger three times to make three quick High G's finishing on High A.

The Triple Strike typically begins and ends on the strikes note and does not go any higher or lower on the scale.

G Triple Strikes

G Triple Strikes on Low A

Low G – G Triple Strike on Low A

    1) Play Low G.
    2) Do a G gracenote to Low A.
    3) Tap your Low A finger three times to make three quick Low G's finishing on Low A.

Low A – G Triple Strike on Low A

    1) Play Low A.
    2) Do a G gracenote while on Low A.
    3) Tap your Low A finger three times to make three quick Low G's finishing on Low A.

B – G Triple Strike on Low A

    3) Play a B.
    4) Do a G gracenote to Low A.
    5) Tap your Low A finger three times to make three quick Low G's finishing on Low A.

C – G Triple Strike on Low A

    1) Play a C.
    2) Do a G gracenote to Low A.
    3) Tap your Low A finger three times to make three quick Low G's finishing on Low A.

D – G Triple Strike on Low A

    1) Play a D.
    2) Do a G gracenote to Low A.
    3) Tap your Low A finger three times to make three quick Low G's finishing on Low A.

E – G Triple Strike on Low A

1) Play an E.
2) Do a G gracenote to Low A.
3) Tap your Low A finger three times to make three quick Low G's finishing on Low A.

F – G Triple Strike on Low A

1) Play an F.
2) Do a G gracenote to Low A.
3) Tap your Low A finger three times to make three quick Low G's finishing on Low A.

The G Triple Strike on Low A can be played on any note from Low G to F but it always ends on Low A.

G Triple Strike on B

Low G – G Triple Strike on B

1) Play Low G.
2) Do a G gracenote to B.
3) Tap your Low A and B fingers three times to make three quick Low G's finishing on a B.

Low A – G Triple Strike on B

1) Play Low A.
2) Do a G gracenote to B.
3) Tap your Low A and B finger three times to make three quick Low G's finishing on a B.

B – G Triple Strike on B

1) Play a B.
2) Do a G gracenote while on B.
3) Tap your Low A and B fingers three times to make three quick Low G's finishing on a B.

C – G Triple Strike on B

1) Play a C.
2) Do a G gracenote to B.
3) Tap your Low A and B fingers three times to make three quick Low G's finishing on a B.

D – G Triple Strike on B

1) Play a D.
2) Do a G gracenote to B.
3) Tap your Low A and B fingers three times to make three quick Low G's finishing on a B.

E – G Triple Strike on B

1) Play an E.
2) Do a G gracenote to B.
3) Tap your Low A and B fingers three times to make three quick Low G's finishing on a B.

F – G Triple Strike on B

1) Play an F.
2) Do a G gracenote to B.
3) Tap your Low A and B fingers three times to make three quick Low G's finishing on a B.

The G Triple Strike on B can be played on any note from Low G to F but it always ends on a B.

G Triple Strike on C

Low G – G Triple Strike on C

1) Play Low G.
2) Do a G gracenote to C.
3) Tap your B and C fingers three times to make three quick Low G's finishing on a B.

Low A – G Triple Strike on C

1) Play Low A.
2) Do a G gracenote to C.
3) Tap your B and C fingers three times to make three quick Low G's finishing on a B.

B – G Triple Strike on C

1) Play a B.
2) Do a G gracenote to C.
3) Tap your B and C fingers three times to make three quick Low G's finishing on a B.

C – G Triple Strike on C

1) Play a C.
2) Do a G gracenote while still on C.
3) Tap your B and C fingers three times to make three quick Low G's finishing on a B.

D – G Triple Strike on C

1) Play a D.
2) Do a G gracenote to C.
3) Tap your B and C fingers three times to make three quick Low G's finishing on a B.

E – G Triple Strike on C

1) Play an E.
2) Do a G gracenote to C.
3) Tap your B and C fingers three times to make three quick Low G's finishing on a B.

F – G Triple Strike on C

1) Play an F.
2) Do a G gracenote to C.
3) Tap your B and C fingers three times to make three quick Low G's finishing on a B.

The G Triple Strike on C can be played on any note from Low G to F but it always ends on a C.

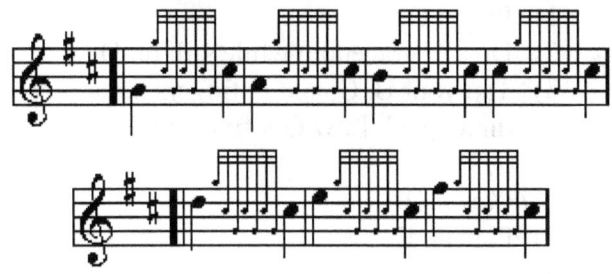

G Triple Strike on D

Low G – G Triple Strike on D

1) Play Low G.
2) Do a G gracenote to D.
3) Tap your B, C, and D fingers three times to make three quick Low G's finishing on a D.

Low A – G Triple Strike on D

1) Play Low A.
2) Do a G gracenote to D.
3) Tap your B, C, and D fingers three times to make three quick Low G's finishing on a D.

B – G Triple Strike on D

1) Play a B.
2) Do a G gracenote to D.
3) Tap your B, C, and D fingers three times to make three quick Low G's finishing on a D.

C – G Triple Strike on D

1) Play a C.
2) Do a G gracenote to D.
3) Tap your B, C, and D fingers three times to make three quick Low G's finishing on a D.

D – G Triple Strike on D

1) Play a D.
2) Do a G gracenote while still on D.
3) Tap your B, C, and D fingers three times to make three quick Low G's finishing on a D.

E – G Triple Strike on D

1) Play an E.
2) Do a G gracenote to D.
3) Tap your B, C, and D fingers three times to make three quick Low G's finishing on a D.

F – G Triple Strike on D

1) Play an F.
2) Do a G gracenote to D.
3) Tap your B, C, and D fingers three times to make three quick Low G's finishing on a D.

The G Triple Strike on D can be played on any note from Low G to F but it always ends on a D.

G Triple Strike to D with a C

Low G – G Triple Strike to D with a C

1) Play Low G.
2) Do a G gracenote to D.
3) Tap your D finger three times to make three quick C's finishing on a D.

Low A – G Triple Strike to D with a C

1) Play Low A.
2) Do a G gracenote to D.
3) Tap your D finger three times to make three quick C's finishing on a D.

B – G Triple Strike to D with a C

1) Play a B.
2) Do a G gracenote to D.
3) Tap your D finger three times to make three quick C's finishing on a D.

C – G Triple Strike to D with a C

1) Play a C.
2) Do a G gracenote to D.
3) Tap your D finger three times to make three quick C's finishing on a D.

D – G Triple Strike to D with a C

1) Play a D.
2) Do a G gracenote while on D.
3) Tap your D finger three times to make three quick C's finishing on a D.

E – G Triple Strike to D with a C

1) Play an E.
2) Do a G gracenote to D.
3) Tap your D finger three times to make three quick C's finishing on a D.

F – G Triple Strike to D with a C

1) Play an F.
2) Do a G gracenote to D.
3) Tap your D finger three times to make three quick C's finishing on a D.

The G Triple Strike on D with a C can be played on any note from Low G to F but it always ends on a D.

G Triple Strike on E

Low G – G Triple Strike on E

1) Play Low G.
2) Do a G gracenote to E.
3) Tap your E finger three times to make three quick Low A's finishing on a D.

Low A – G Triple Strike on E

1) Play Low A.
2) Do a G gracenote to E.
3) Tap your E finger three times to make three quick Low A's finishing on a D.

B – G Triple Strike on E

1) Play a B.
2) Do a G gracenote to E.
3) Tap your E finger three times to make three quick Low A's finishing on a D.

C – G Triple Strike on E

1) Play a C.
2) Do a G gracenote to E.
3) Tap your E finger three times to make three quick Low A's finishing on a D.

D – G Triple Strike on E

1) Play a D.
2) Do a G gracenote to E.
3) Tap your E finger three times to make three quick Low A's finishing on a D.

E – G Triple Strike on E

1) Play an E.
2) Do a G gracenote while on E.
3) Tap your E finger three times to make three quick Low A's finishing on a D.

F – G Triple Strike on E

1) Play an F.
2) Do a G gracenote to E.
3) Tap your E finger three times to make three quick Low A's finishing on a D.

The G Triple Strike on E can be played on any note from Low G to F but it always ends on an E.

G Triple Strike on F

Low G – G Triple Strike on F

1) Play Low G.
2) Do a G gracenote to F.
3) Tap your F finger three times to make three quick E's finishing on a D.

Low A – G Triple Strike on F

1) Play Low A.
2) Do a G gracenote to F.
3) Tap your F finger three times to make three quick E's finishing on a D.

B – G Triple Strike on F

1) Play a B.
2) Do a G gracenote to F.
3) Tap your F finger three times to make three quick E's finishing on a D.

C – G Triple Strike on F

1) Play a C.
2) Do a G gracenote to F.
3) Tap your F finger three times to make three quick E's finishing on a D.

D – G Triple Strike on F

1) Play a D.
2) Do a G gracenote to F.
3) Tap your F finger three times to make three quick E's finishing on a D.

E – G Triple Strike on F

1) Play an E.
2) Do a G gracenote to F.
3) Tap your F finger three times to make three quick E's finishing on a D.

F – G Triple Strike on F

1) Play an F.
2) Do a G while on F.
3) Tap your F finger three times to make three quick E's finishing on a D.

The G Triple Strike on F can be played on any note from Low G to F but it always ends on an F.

Thumb Triple Strikes

Thumb Triple Strike on Low A

Low G – Thumb Triple Strike on Low A

1) Play Low G.
2) Play High A.
3) Play Low A.
4) Tap your Low A finger three times to make three quick Low G's finishing on a Low A.

Low A – Thumb Triple Strike on Low A

1) Play Low A.
2) Play High A.
3) Play Low A again.
4) Tap your Low A finger three times to make three quick Low G's finishing on a Low A.

B – Thumb Triple Strike on Low A

1) Play a B.
2) Play High A.
3) Play Low A.
4) Tap your Low A finger three times to make three quick Low G's finishing on a Low A.

C – Thumb Triple Strike on Low A

1) Play a C.
2) Play High A.
3) Play Low A.
4) Tap your Low A finger three times to make three quick Low G's finishing on a Low A.

D – Thumb Triple Strike on Low A

1) Play a D.
2) Play High A.
3) Play Low A.
4) Tap your Low A finger three times to make three quick Low G's finishing on a Low A.

E – Thumb Triple Strike on Low A

1) Play an E.
2) Play High A.
3) Play Low A.
4) Tap your Low A finger three times to make three quick Low G's finishing on a Low A.

F – Thumb Triple Strike on Low A

1) Play an F.
2) Play High A.
3) Play Low A.
4) Tap your Low A finger three times to make three quick Low G's finishing on a Low A.

High G – Thumb Triple Strike on Low A

1) Play High G.
2) Play High A.
3) Play Low A.
4) Tap your Low A finger three times to make three quick Low G's finishing on a Low A.

The Thumb Triple Strike on Low A can be played on any note from Low G to High G but it always ends on a Low A.

Thumb Triple Strike on B

Low G – Thumb Triple Strike on B

1) Play Low G.
2) Play High A.
3) Play a B.
4) Tap your Low A and B fingers three times to make three quick Low G's finishing on a B.

Low A – Thumb Triple Strike on B

1) Play Low A.
2) Play High A.
3) Play a B.
4) Tap your Low A and B fingers three times to make three quick Low G's finishing on a B.

B – Thumb Triple Strike on B

1) Play a B.
2) Play High A.
3) Play a B again.
4) Tap your Low A and B fingers three times to make three quick Low G's finishing on a B.

C – Thumb Triple Strike on B

1) Play a C.
2) Play High A.
3) Play a B again.
4) Tap your Low A and B fingers three times to make three quick Low G's finishing on a B.

D – Thumb Triple Strike on B

1) Play a D.
2) Play High A.
3) Play a B.
4) Tap your Low A and B fingers three times to make three quick Low G's finishing on a B.

E – Thumb Triple Strike on B

1) Play an E.
2) Play High A.
3) Play a B.
4) Tap your Low A and B fingers three times to make three quick Low G's finishing on a B.

F – Thumb Triple Strike on B

1) Play an F.
2) Play High A.
3) Play a B.
4) Tap your Low A and B fingers three times to make three quick Low G's finishing on a B.

High G – Thumb Strike on B

1) Play High G.
2) Play High A.
3) Play a B.
4) Tap your Low A and B fingers three times to make three quick Low G's finishing on a B.

The Thumb Triple Strike on B can be played on any note from Low G to High G but it always ends on a B.

Thumb Triple Strike on C

Low G – Thumb Triple Strike on C

1) Play Low G.
2) Play High A.
3) Play a C.
4) Tap your B and C fingers three times to make three quick Low G's finishing on a C.

Low A – Thumb Triple Strike on C

1) Play Low A.
2) Play High A.
3) Play a C.
4) Tap your B and C fingers three times to make three quick Low G's finishing on a C.

B – Thumb Triple Strike on C

1) Play a B.
2) Play High A.
3) Play a C.
4) Tap your B and C fingers three times to make three quick Low G's finishing on a C.

C – Thumb Triple Strike on C

1) Play a C.
2) Play High A.
3) Play a C again.
4) Tap your B and C fingers three times to make three quick Low G's finishing on a C.

D – Thumb Triple Strike on C

1) Play a D.
2) Play High A.
3) Play a C.
4) Tap your B and C fingers three times to make three quick Low G's finishing on a C.

E – Thumb Triple Strike on C

1) Play an E.
2) Play High A.
3) Play a C.
4) Tap your B and C fingers three times to make three quick Low G's finishing on a C.

F – Thumb Triple Strike on C

1) Play an F.
2) Play High A.
3) Play a C.
4) Tap your B and C fingers three times to make three quick Low G's finishing on a C.

High G – Thumb Triple Strike on C

1) Play High G.
2) Play High A.
3) Play a C.
4) Tap your B and C fingers three times to make three quick Low G's finishing on a C.

The Thumb Triple Strike on C can be played on any note from Low G to High G but it always ends on a C.

Thumb Triple Strike on D

Low G – Thumb Triple Strike on D

1) Play Low G.
2) Play High A.
3) Play a D.
4) Tap your B, C, and D fingers three times to make three quick Low G's finishing on a D.

Low A – Thumb Triple Strike on D

1) Play Low A.
2) Play High A.
3) Play a D.
4) Tap your B, C, and D fingers three times to make three quick Low G's finishing on a D.

B – Thumb Triple Strike on D

1) Play a B.
2) Play High A.
3) Play a D.
4) Tap your B, C, and D fingers three times to make three quick Low G's finishing on a D.

C – Thumb Triple Strike on D

1) Play a C.
2) Play High A.
3) Play a D.
4) Tap your B, C, and D fingers three times to make three quick Low G's finishing on a D.

D – Thumb Triple Strike on D

1) Play a D.
2) Play High A.
3) Play a D again.
4) Tap your B, C, and D fingers three times to make three quick Low G's finishing on a D.

E – Thumb Triple Strike on D

1) Play an E.
2) Play High A.
3) Play a D.
4) Tap your B, C, and D fingers three times to make three quick Low G's finishing on a D.

F – Thumb Triple Strike on D

1) Play an F.
2) Play High A.
3) Play a D.
4) Tap your B, C, and D fingers three times to make three quick Low G's finishing on a D.

High G – Thumb Triple Strike on D

1) Play High G.
2) Play High A.
3) Play a D.
4) Tap your B, C, and D fingers three times to make three quick Low G's finishing on a D.

The Thumb Triple Strike on D can be played on any note from Low G to High G but it always ends on a D.

Thumb Triple Strike on D with a C

Low G – Thumb Triple Strike on D with a C

1) Play Low G.
2) Play High A.
3) Play a D.
4) Tap your D finger three times to make three quick C's finishing on a D.

Low A – Thumb Triple Strike on D with a C

1) Play Low A.
2) Play High A.
3) Play a D.
4) Tap your D finger three times to make three quick C's finishing on a D.

B – Thumb Triple Strike on D with a C

1) Play a B.
2) Play High A.
3) Play a D.
4) Tap your D finger three times to make three quick C's finishing on a D.

C – Thumb Triple Strike on D with a C

1) Play a C.
2) Play High A.
3) Play a D.
4) Tap your D finger three times to make three quick C's finishing on a D.

D – Thumb Triple Strike on D with a C

    1) Play a D.
    2) Play High A.
    3) Play a D again.
    4) Tap your D finger three times to make three quick C's finishing on a D.

E – Thumb Triple Strike on D with a C

    1) Play an E.
    2) Play High A.
    3) Play a D.
    4) Tap your D finger three times to make three quick C's finishing on a D.

F – Thumb Triple Strike on D with a C

    1) Play an F.
    2) Play High A.
    3) Play a D.
    4) Tap your D finger three times to make three quick C's finishing on a D.

High G – Thumb Triple Strike on D with a C

    1) Play High G.
    2) Play High A.
    3) Play a D.
    4) Tap your D finger three times to make three quick C's finishing on a D.

The Thumb Triple Strike on D with a C can be played on any note from Low G to High G but it always ends on a D.

Thumb Triple Strike on E

Low G – Thumb Triple Strike on E

1) Play Low G.
2) Play High A.
3) Play an E.
4) Tap your E finger three times to make three quick Low A's finishing on an E.

Low A – Thumb Triple Strike on E

1) Play Low A.
2) Play High A.
3) Play an E.
4) Tap your E finger three times to make three quick Low A's finishing on an E.

B – Thumb Triple Strike on E

1) Play a B.
2) Play High A.
3) Play an E.
4) Tap your E finger three times to make three quick Low A's finishing on an E.

C – Thumb Triple Strike on E

1) Play a C.
2) Play High A.
3) Play an E.
4) Tap your E finger three times to make three quick Low A's finishing on an E.

D – Thumb Triple Strike on E

1) Play a D.
2) Play High A.
3) Play an E.
4) Tap your E finger three times to make three quick Low A's finishing on an E.

E – Thumb Triple Strike on E

1) Play an E.
2) Play High A.
3) Play an E again.
4) Tap your E finger three times to make three quick Low A's finishing on an E.

F – Thumb Triple Strike on E

1) Play an F.
2) Play High A.
3) Play an E.
4) Tap your E finger three times to make three quick Low A's finishing on an E.

High G – Thumb Triple Strike on E

1) Play High G.
2) Play High A.
3) Play an E.
4) Tap your E finger three times to make three quick Low A's finishing on an E.

The Thumb Triple Strike on E can be played on any note from Low G to High G but it always ends on an E.

Thumb Triple Strike on F

Low G – Thumb Triple Strike on F

1) Play Low G.
2) Play High A.
3) Play an F.
4) Tap your F finger three times to make three quick E's finishing on an F.

Low A – Thumb Triple Strike on F

1) Play Low A.
2) Play High A.
3) Play an F.
4) Tap your F finger three times to make three quick E's finishing on an F.

B – Thumb Triple Strike on F

1) Play a B.
2) Play High A.
3) Play an F.
4) Tap your F finger three times to make three quick E's finishing on an F.

C – Thumb Triple Strike on F

1) Play a C.
2) Play High A.
3) Play an F.
4) Tap your F finger three times to make three quick E's finishing on an F.

D – Thumb Triple Strike on F

1) Play a D.
2) Play High A.
3) Play an F.
4) Tap your F finger three times to make three quick E's finishing on an F.

E – Thumb Triple Strike on F

1) Play an E.
2) Play High A.
3) Play an F.
4) Tap your F finger three times to make three quick E's finishing on an F.

F – Thumb Triple Strike on F

1) Play an F.
2) Play High A.
3) Play an F again.
4) Tap your F finger three times to make three quick E's finishing on an F.

High G – Thumb Triple Strike on F

1) Play High G.
2) Play High A.
3) Play an F.
4) Tap your F finger three times to make three quick E's finishing on an F.

The Thumb Triple Strike on F can be played on any note from Low G to High G but it always ends on an F.

Thumb Triple Strike on High G

Low G – Thumb Triple Strike on High G

1) Play Low G.
2) Play High A.
3) Play High G.
4) Tap your G finger three times to make three quick F's finishing on a High G.

Low A – Thumb Triple Strike on High G

1) Play Low A.
2) Play High A.
3) Play High G.
4) Tap your G finger three times to make three quick F's finishing on a High G.

B – Thumb Triple Strike on High G

1) Play a B.
2) Play High A.
3) Play High G.
4) Tap your G finger three times to make three quick F's finishing on a High G.

C – Thumb Triple Strike on High G

1) Play a C.
2) Play High A.
3) Play High G.
4) Tap your G finger three times to make three quick F's finishing on a High G.

D – Thumb Triple Strike on High G

1) Play a D.
2) Play High A.
3) Play High G.
4) Tap your G finger three times to make three quick F's finishing on a High G.

E – Thumb Triple Strike on High G

1) Play an E.
2) Play High A.
3) Play High G.
4) Tap your G finger three times to make three quick F's finishing on a High G.

F – Thumb Triple Strike on High G

1) Play an F.
2) Play High A.
3) Play High G.
4) Tap your G finger three times to make three quick F's finishing on a High G.

High G – Thumb Triple Strike on High G

1) Play High G.
2) Play High A.
3) Play High G again.
4) Tap your G finger three times to make three quick F's finishing on a High G.

The Thumb Triple Strike on High G can be played on any note from Low G to High G but it always ends on High G.

Half Triple Strikes

Half Triple Strike on Low A

Low G – Half Triple Strike on Low A

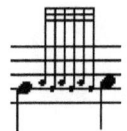

1) Play Low G.
2) Play Low A.
3) Tap your Low A finger three times to make three quick Low G's finishing on a Low A.

Low A – Half Triple Strike on Low A

1) Play Low A.
2) Tap your Low A finger three times to make three quick Low G's finishing on a Low A.

B – Half Triple Strike on Low A

1) Play a B.
2) Play Low A.
3) Tap your Low A finger three times to make three quick Low G's finishing on a Low A.

C – Half Triple Strike on Low A

1) Play a C.
2) Play Low A.
3) Tap your Low A finger three times to make three quick Low G's finishing on Low A.

D – Half Triple Strike on Low A

1) Play a D.
2) Play Low A.
3) Tap your Low A finger three times to make three quick Low G's finishing on Low A.

E – Half Triple Strike on Low A

1) Play an E.
2) Play Low A.
3) Tap your Low A finger three times to make three quick Low G's finishing on a Low A.

F – Half Triple Strike on Low A

1) Play an F.
2) Play Low A.
3) Tap your Low A finger three times to make three quick Low G's finishing on a Low A.

High G – Half Triple Strike on Low A

1) Play High G.
2) Play Low A.
3) Tap your Low A finger three times to make three quick Low G's finishing on a Low A.

High A – Half Triple Strike on Low A

1) Play High A.
2) Play Low A.
3) Tap your Low A finger three times to make three quick Low G's finishing on a Low A.

The Thumb Triple Strike on Low A can be played on any note from Low G to High A but it always ends on Low A.

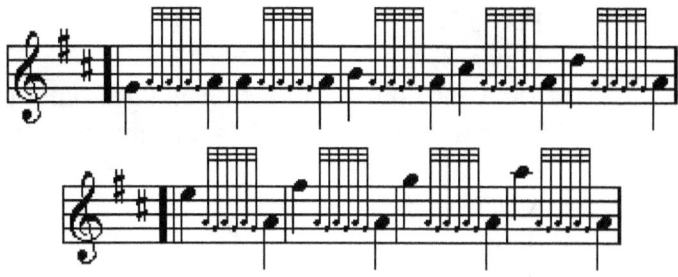

315

Half Triple Strike on B

Low G – Half Triple Strike on B

1) Play Low G.
2) Play a B.
3) Tap your Low A and B fingers three times to make three quick Low G's finishing on a B.

Low A – Half Triple Strike on B

1) Play Low A.
2) Play a B.
3) Tap your Low A and B fingers three times to make three quick Low G's finishing on a B.

B – Half Triple Strike on B

1) Play a B.
2) Tap your Low A and B fingers three times to make three quick Low G's finishing on a B.

C – Half Triple Strike on B

1) Play a C.
2) Play a B.
3) Tap your Low A and B fingers three times to make three quick Low G's finishing on a B.

D – Half Triple Strike on B

1) Play a D.
2) Play a B.
3) Tap your Low A and B fingers three times to make three quick Low G's finishing on a B.

E – Half Triple Strike on B

1) Play an E.
2) Play a B.
3) Tap your Low A and B fingers three times to make three quick Low G's finishing on a B.

F – Half Triple Strike on B

1) Play an F.
2) Play a B.
3) Tap your Low A and B fingers three times to make three quick Low G's finishing on a B.

High G – Half Triple Strike on B

1) Play High G.
2) Play a B.
3) Tap your Low A and B fingers three times to make three quick Low G's finishing on a B.

High A – Half Triple Strike on B

1) Play High A.
2) Play a B.
3) Tap your Low A and B fingers three times to make three quick Low G's finishing on a B.

The Thumb Triple Strike on B can be played on any note from Low G to High A but it always ends on a B.

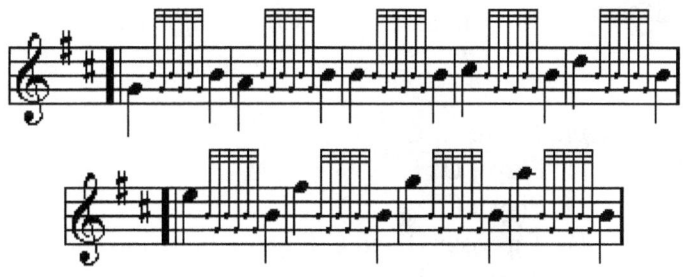

Half Triple Strike on C

Low G – Half Triple Strike on C

1) Play Low G.
2) Play a C.
3) Tap your B and C fingers three times to make three quick Low G's finishing on a C.

Low A – Half Triple Strike on C

1) Play Low A.
2) Play a C.
3) Tap your B and C fingers three times to make three quick Low G's finishing on a C.

B – Half Triple Strike on C

1) Play a B.
2) Play a C.
3) Tap your B and C fingers three times to make three quick Low G's finishing on a C.

C – Half Triple Strike on C

1) Play a C.
2) Tap your B and C fingers three times to make three quick Low G's finishing on a C.

D – Half Triple Strike on C

1) Play a D.
2) Play a C.
3) Tap your B and C fingers three times to make three quick Low G's finishing on a C.

E – Half Triple Strike on C

1) Play an E.
2) Play a C.
3) Tap your B and C fingers three times to make three quick Low G's finishing on a C.

F – Half Triple Strike on C

1) Play an F.
2) Play a C.
3) Tap your B and C fingers three times to make three quick Low G's finishing on a C.

High G – Half Triple Strike on C

1) Play High G.
2) Play a C.
3) Tap your B and C fingers three times to make three quick Low G's finishing on a C.

High A – Half Triple Strike on C

1) Play High A.
2) Play a C.
3) Tap your B and C fingers three times to make three quick Low G's finishing on a C.

The Thumb Triple Strike on C can be played on any note from Low G to High A but it always ends on a C.

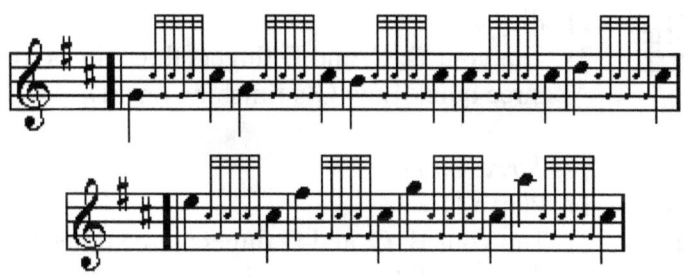

Half Triple Strike on D

Low G – Half Triple Strike on D

1) Play Low G.
2) Play a D.
3) Tap your B, C, and D fingers three times to make three quick Low G's finishing on a D.

Low A – Half Triple Strike on D

1) Play Low A.
2) Play a D.
3) Tap your B, C, and D fingers three times to make three quick Low G's finishing on a D.

B – Half Triple Strike on D

1) Play a B.
2) Play a D.
3) Tap your B, C, and D fingers three times to make three quick Low G's finishing on a D.

C – Half Triple Strike on D

1) Play a C.
2) Play a D.
3) Tap your B, C, and D fingers three times to make three quick Low G's finishing on a D.

D – Half Triple Strike on D

1) Play a D.
2) Tap your B, C, and D fingers three times to make three quick Low G's finishing on a D.

E – Half Triple Strike on D

1) Play an E.
2) Play a D.
3) Tap your B, C, and D fingers three times to make three quick Low G's finishing on a D.

F – Half Triple Strike on D

1) Play an F.
2) Play a D.
3) Tap your B, C, and D fingers three times to make three quick Low G's finishing on a D.

High G – Half Triple Strike on D

1) Play High G.
2) Play a D.
3) Tap your B, C, and D fingers three times to make three quick Low G's finishing on a D.

High A – Half Triple Strike on D

1) Play High A.
2) Play a D.
3) Tap your B, C, and D fingers three times to make three quick Low G's finishing on a D.

The Thumb Triple Strike on D can be played on any note from Low G to High A but it always ends on a D.

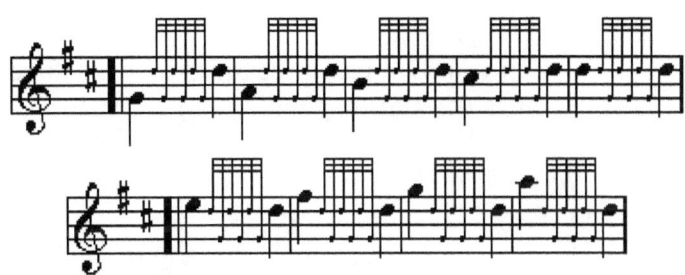

Half Triple Strike on D with a C

Low G – Half Triple Strike on D with a C

1) Play Low G.
2) Play a D.
3) Tap your D finger three times to make three quick C's finishing on a D.

Low A – Half Triple Strike on D with a C

1) Play Low A.
2) Play a D.
3) Tap your D finger three times to make three quick C's finishing on a D.

B – Half Triple Strike on D with a C

1) Play a B.
2) Play a D.
3) Tap your D finger three times to make three quick C's finishing on a D.

C – Half Triple Strike on D with a C

1) Play a C.
2) Play a D.
3) Tap your D finger three times to make three quick C's finishing on a D.

D – Half Triple Strike on D with a C

1) Play a D.
2) Tap your D finger three times to make three quick C's finishing on a D.

E – Half Triple Strike on D with a C

1) Play an E.
2) Play a D.
3) Tap your D finger three times to make three quick C's finishing on a D.

F – Half Triple Strike on D with a C

1) Play an F.
2) Play a D.
3) Tap your D finger three times to make three quick C's finishing on a D.

High G – Half Triple Strike on D with a C

1) Play High G.
2) Play a D.
3) Tap your D finger three times to make three quick C's finishing on a D.

High A – Half Triple Strike on D with a C

1) Play High A.
2) Play a D.
3) Tap your D finger three times to make three quick C's finishing on a D.

The Thumb Triple Strike on D with a C can be played on any note from Low G to High A but it always ends on a D.

Half Triple Strike on E

Low G – Half Triple Strike on E

1) Play Low G.
2) Play an E.
3) Tap your E finger three times to make three quick Low A's finishing on an E.

Low A – Half Triple Strike on E

1) Play Low A.
2) Play an E.
3) Tap your E finger three times to make three quick Low A's finishing on an E.

B – Half Triple Strike on E

1) Play a B.
2) Play an E.
3) Tap your E finger three times to make three quick Low A's finishing on an E.

C – Half Triple Strike on E

1) Play a C.
2) Play an E.
3) Tap your E finger three times to make three quick Low A's finishing on an E.

D – Half Triple Strike on E

1) Play a D.
2) Play an E.
3) Tap your E finger three times to make three quick Low A's finishing on an E.

E – Half Triple Strike on E

1) Play an E.
2) Tap your E finger three times to make three quick Low A's finishing on an E.

F – Half Triple Strike on E

    1) Play an F.
    2) Play an E.
    3) Tap your E finger three times to make three quick Low A's finishing on an E.

High G – Half Triple Strike on E

    1) Play High G.
    2) Play an E.
    3) Tap your E finger three times to make three quick Low A's finishing on an E.

High A – Half Triple Strike on E

    1) Play High A.
    2) Play an E.
    3) Tap your E finger three times to make three quick Low A's finishing on an E.

The Thumb Triple Strike on E can be played on any note from Low G to High A but it always ends on an E.

Half Triple Strike on F

Low G – Half Triple Strike on F

1) Play Low G.
2) Play an F.
3) Tap your F finger three times making three quick E's finishing on an F.

Low A – Half Triple Strike on F

1) Play Low A.
2) Play an F.
3) Tap your F finger three times making three quick E's finishing on an F.

B – Half Triple Strike on F

1) Play a B.
2) Play an F.
3) Tap your F finger three times making three quick E's finishing on an F.

C – Half Triple Strike on F

1) Play a C.
2) Play an F.
3) Tap your F finger three times making three quick E's finishing on an F.

D – Half Triple Strike on F

1) Play a D.
2) Play an F.
3) Tap your F finger three times making three quick E's finishing on an F.

E – Half Triple Strike on F

1) Play an E.
2) Play an F.
3) Tap your F finger three times making three quick E's finishing on an F.

F – Half Triple Strike on F

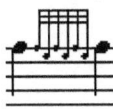
1) Play an F.
2) Tap your F finger three times making three quick E's finishing on an F.

High G – Half Triple Strike on F

1) Play High G.
2) Play an F.
3) Tap your F finger three times making three quick E's finishing on an F.

High A – Half Triple Strike on F

1) Play High A.
2) Play an F.
3) Tap your F finger three times making three quick E's finishing on an F.

The Thumb Triple Strike on F can be played on any note from Low G to High A but it always ends on an F.

Half Triple Strike on High G

Low G – Half Triple Strike on High G

1) Play Low G.
2) Play High G.
3) Tap your G finger three times making three quick F's finishing on High G.

Low A – Half Triple Strike on High G

1) Play Low A.
2) Play High G.
3) Tap your G finger three times making three quick F's finishing on High G.

B – Half Triple Strike on High G

1) Play a B.
2) Play High G.
3) Tap your G finger three times making three quick F's finishing on High G.

C – Half Triple Strike on High G

1) Play a C.
2) Play High G.
3) Tap your G finger three times making three quick F's finishing on High G.

D – Half Triple Strike on High G

1) Play a D.
2) Play High G.
3) Tap your G finger three times making three quick F's finishing on High G.

E – Half Triple Strike on High G

1) Play an E.
2) Play High G.
3) Tap your G finger three times making three quick F's finishing on High G.

F – Half Triple Strike on High G

1) Play an F.
2) Play High G.
3) Tap your G finger three times making three quick F's finishing on High G.

High G – Half Triple Strike on High G

1) Play High G.
2) Tap your G finger three times making three quick F's finishing on High G.

High A – Half Triple Strike on High G

1) Play High A.
2) Play High G.
3) Tap your G finger three times making three quick F's finishing on High G.

The Thumb Triple Strike on High G can be played on any note from Low G to High A but it always ends on High G.

Half Triple Strike on High A

Low G – Half Triple Strike on High A

1) Play Low G.
2) Play High A.
3) Brush your thumb across the High A hole three times making three quick High G's finishing on High A.

Low A – Half Triple Strike on High A

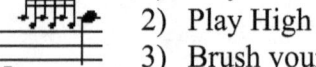

1) Play Low A.
2) Play High A.
3) Brush your thumb across the High A hole three times making three quick High G's finishing on High A.

B – Half Triple Strike on High A

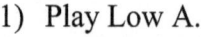

1) Play a B.
2) Play High A.
3) Brush your thumb across the High A hole three times making three quick High G's finishing on High A.

C – Half Triple Strike on High A

1) Play a C.
2) Play High A.
3) Brush your thumb across the High A hole three times making three quick High G's finishing on High A.

D – Half Triple Strike on High A

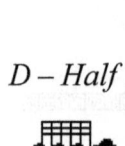

1) Play a D.
2) Play High A.
3) Brush your thumb across the High A hole three times making three quick High G's finishing on High A.

E – Half Triple Strike on High A

1) Play an E.
2) Play High A.
3) Brush your thumb across the High A hole three times making three quick High G's finishing on High A.

F – Half Triple Strike on High A

1) Play an F.
2) Play High A.
3) Brush your thumb across the High A hole three times making three quick High G's finishing on High A.

High G – Half Triple Strike on High A

1) Play High G.
2) Play High A.
3) Brush your thumb across the High A hole three times making three quick High G's finishing on High A.

High A – Half Triple Strike on High A

1) Play High A.
2) Brush your thumb across the High A hole three times making three quick High G's finishing on High A.

The Thumb Triple Strike on High A can be played on any note from Low G to High A but it always ends on High A.

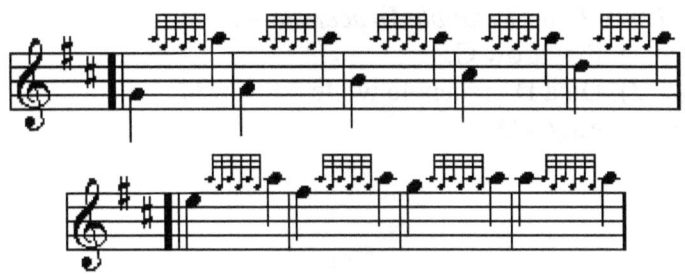

Double Gracenotes

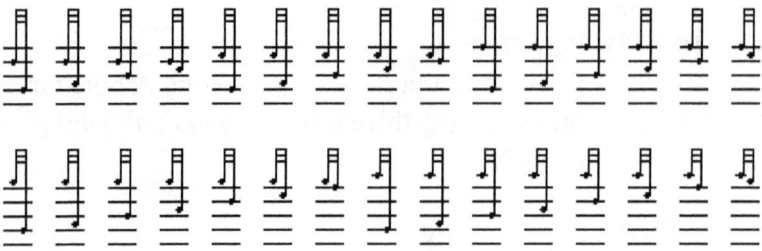

D Double Gracenotes

Low G – D, Low G Double Gracenote – Low A
1) Play Low G.
2) Do a D gracenote while on Low G.
3) Play Low A.

Low G – D, Low G Double Gracenote – B
1) Play Low G.
2) Do a D gracenote while on Low G.
3) Play a B.

Low G – D, Low G Double Gracenote – C
1) Play Low G.
2) Do a D gracenote while on Low G.
3) Play a C.

Low G – D, Low G Double Gracenote – D
1) Play Low G.
2) Do a D gracenote while on Low G.
3) Play a D.

Low A – D, Low G Double Gracenote – Low A
1) Play Low A.
2) Do a D gracenote while on Low A.
3) Do a Strike to Low G finishing on Low A.

Low A – D, Low G Double Gracenote – B
1) Play Low A.
2) Do a D gracenote while on Low A.
3) Do a Strike to Low G finishing on a B.

Low A – D, Low G Double Gracenote – C
1) Play Low A.
2) Do a D gracenote while on Low A.
3) Do a Strike to Low G finishing on a C.

Low A – D, Low G Double Gracenote – D
1) Play Low A.
2) Do a D gracenote while on Low A.
3) Do a Strike to Low G finishing on a D.

B – D, Low G Double Gracenote – Low A
1) Play a B.
2) Do a D gracenote while on B.
3) Do a Strike to Low G finishing on a Low A.

B – D, Low G Double Gracenote – B
1) Play a B.
2) Do a D gracenote while on B.
3) Do a Strike to Low G finishing on a B.

B – D, Low G Double Gracenote – C
1) Play a B.
2) Do a D gracenote while on B.
3) Do a Strike to Low G finishing on a C.

B – D, Low G Double Gracenote – D
1) Play a B.
2) Do a D gracenote while on B.
3) Do a Strike to Low G finishing on a D.

C – D, Low G Double Gracenote – Low A
1) Play a C.
2) Do a D gracenote while on C.
3) Do a Strike to Low G finishing on a Low A.

C – D, Low G Double Gracenote – B
1) Play a C.
2) Do a D gracenote while on C.
3) Do a Strike to Low G finishing on a B.

C – D, Low G Double Gracenote – C
1) Play a C.
2) Do a D gracenote while on C.
3) Do a Strike to Low G while still on C.

C – D, Low G Double Gracenote – D
1) Play a C.
2) Do a D gracenote while on C.
3) Do a Strike to Low G finishing on a D.

Low A – D, Low A Double Gracenote – B
1) Play Low A.
2) Do a D gracenote while on Low A.
3) Play a B.

Low A – D, Low A Double Gracenote – C
1) Play Low A.
2) Do a D gracenote while on Low A.
3) Play a C.

Low A – D, Low A Double Gracenote – D
1) Play Low A.
2) Do a D gracenote while on Low A.
3) Play a D.

B – D, Low A Double Gracenote – B
1) Play a B.
2) Do a D gracenote while on B.
3) Do a Strike to Low A while on B.

B – D, Low A Double Gracenote – C
1) Play a B.
2) Do a D gracenote while on B.
3) Do a Strike to Low A finishing on C.

B – D, Low A Double Gracenote – D
1) Play a B.
2) Do a D gracenote while on B.
3) Do a Strike to Low A finishing on a D.

C – D, Low A Double Gracenote – B
1) Play a C.
2) Do a D gracenote while on C.
3) Do a Strike to Low A finishing on a B.

C – D, Low A Double Gracenote – C
1) Play a C.
2) Do a D gracenote while on C.
3) Do a Strike to Low A while still on C.

C – D, Low A Double Gracenote – D
1) Play a C.
2) Do a D gracenote while on C.
3) Do a Strike to Low A finishing on a D.

B – D, B Double Gracenote – C
1) Play a B.
2) Do a D gracenote while on B.
3) Play a C.

B – D, B Double Gracenote – D
1) Play a B.
2) Do a D gracenote while on B.
3) Play a D.

C – D, B Double Gracenote – B
1) Play a C.
2) Do a D gracenote while on C.
3) Do a Strike to B while still on C.

C – D, B Double Gracenote – D
1) Play a C.
2) Do a D gracenote while on C.
3) Do a Strike to B finishing on a D.

C – D, C Double Gracenote – C
1) Play a C.
2) Do a D gracenote while still on C.
3) Play a D.

The D Double Gracenote is typically played between the first and last note of the embellishment.

E Double Gracenotes

Low G – E, Low G Double Gracenote – Low A
1) Play Low G.
2) Do an E gracenote while on Low G.
3) Play Low A.

Low G – E, Low G Double Gracenote – B
1) Play Low G.
2) Do an E gracenote while on Low G.
3) Play a B.

Low G – E, Low G Double Gracenote – C
1) Play Low G.
2) Do an E gracenote while on Low G.
3) Play a C.

Low G – E, Low G Double Gracenote – D
1) Play Low G.
2) Do an E gracenote while on Low G.
3) Play a D.

Low G – E, Low G Double Gracenote – E
1) Play Low G.
2) Do an E gracenote while on Low G.
3) Play an E.

Low A – E, Low G Double Gracenote – Low A
1) Play Low A.
2) Do an E gracenote while on Low A.
3) Do a Strike to Low G finishing on Low A.

Low A – E, Low G Double Gracenote – B
1) Play Low A.
2) Do an E gracenote while on Low A.
3) Do a Strike to Low G finishing on a B.

Low A – E, Low G Double Gracenote – C
1) Play Low A.
2) Do an E gracenote while on Low A.
3) Do a Strike to Low G finishing on a C.

Low A – E, Low G Double Gracenote – D
1) Play Low A.
2) Do an E gracenote while on Low A.
3) Do a Strike to Low G finishing on a D.

Low A – E, Low G Double Gracenote – E
1) Play Low A.
2) Do an E gracenote while on Low A.
3) Do a Strike to Low G finishing on an E.

B – E, Low G Double Gracenote – Low A
1) Play a B.
2) Do an E gracenote while on a B.
3) Do a Strike to Low G finishing on a Low A.

B – E, Low G Double Gracenote – B
1) Play a B.
2) Do an E gracenote while on B.
3) Do a Strike to Low G while still on B.

B – E, Low G Double Gracenote – C
1) Play a B.
2) Do an E gracenote while on B.
3) Do a Strike to Low G finishing on a C.

B – E, Low G Double Gracenote – D
1) Play a B.
2) Do an E gracenote while on B.
3) Do a Strike to Low G finishing on a D.

B – E, Low G Double Gracenote – E
1) Play a B.
2) Do an E gracenote while on B.
3) Do a Strike to Low G finishing on an E.

C – E, Low G Double Gracenote – Low A
1) Play a C.
2) Do an E gracenote while on C.
3) Do a Strike to Low G finishing on Low A.

C – E, Low G Double Gracenote – B
1) Play a C.
2) Do an E gracenote while on C.
3) Do a Strike to Low G finishing on a B.

C – E, Low G Double Gracenote – C
1) Play a C.
2) Do an E gracenote while on C.
3) Do a Strike to Low G while still on C.

C – E, Low G Double Gracenote – D
1) Play a C.
2) Do an E gracenote while on C.
3) Do a Strike to Low G finishing on a D.

D – E, Low G Double Gracenote – E
1) Play a C.
2) Do an E gracenote while on C.
3) Do a Strike to Low G finishing on an E.

D – E, Low G Double Gracenote – Low A
1) Play a D.
2) Do an E gracenote while on D.
3) Do a Strike to Low G finishing on Low A.

D – E, Low G Double Gracenote – B
1) Play a D.
2) Do an E gracenote while on D.
3) Do a Strike to Low G finishing on a B.

D – E, Low G Double Gracenote – C
1) Play a D.
2) Do an E gracenote while on D.
3) Do a Strike to Low G finishing on a C.

D – E, Low G Double Gracenote – D
1) Play a D.
2) Do an E gracenote while on D.
3) Do a Strike to Low G while still on D.

D – E, Low G Double Gracenote – E
1) Play a D.
2) Do an E gracenote while on D.
3) Do a Strike to Low G finishing on an E.

Low A – E, Low A Double Gracenote – B
1) Play Low A.
2) Do an E gracenote while on Low A.
3) Play a B.

Low A – E, Low A Double Gracenote – C
1) Play Low A.
2) Do an E gracenote while on Low A.
3) Play a C.

Low A – E, Low A Double Gracenote – D
1) Play Low A.
2) Do an E gracenote while on Low A.
3) Play a D.

Low A – E, Low A Double Gracenote – E
1) Play Low A.
2) Do an E gracenote while on Low A.
3) Play an E.

B – E, Low A Double Gracenote – B
1) Play a B.
2) Do an E gracenote while on B.
3) Do a Strike to Low A while still on a B.

B – E, Low A Double Gracenote – C
1) Play a B.
2) Do an E gracenote while on B.
3) Do a Strike to Low A finishing on a C.

B – E, Low A Double Gracenote – D
1) Play a B.
2) Do an E gracenote while on B.
3) Do a Strike to Low A finishing on a D.

B – E, Low A Double Gracenote – E

    1) Play a B.
    2) Do an E gracenote while on B.
    3) Do a Strike to Low A finishing on an E.

C – E, Low A Double Gracenote – B

    1) Play a C.
    2) Do an E gracenote while on C.
    3) Do a Strike to Low A finishing on a B.

C – E, Low A Double Gracenote – C

    1) Play a C.
    2) Do an E gracenote while on C.
    3) Do a Strike to Low A while still on C.

C – E, Low A Double Gracenote – D

    1) Play a C.
    2) Do an E gracenote while on C.
    3) Do a Strike to Low A finishing on a D.

C – E, Low A Double Gracenote – E

    1) Play a C.
    2) Do an E gracenote while on C.
    3) Do a Strike to Low A finishing on an E.

D – E, Low A Double Gracenote – B

    1) Play a D.
    2) Do an E gracenote while on D.
    3) Do a Strike to Low A finishing on a B.

D – E, Low A Double Gracenote – C
   1) Play a D.
   2) Do an E gracenote while on D.
   3) Do a Strike to Low A finishing on a C.

D – E, Low A Double Gracenote – D
   1) Play a D.
   2) Do an E gracenote while on D.
   3) Do a Strike to Low A while still on D.

D – E, Low A Double Gracenote – E
   1) Play a D.
   2) Do an E gracenote while on D.
   3) Do a Strike to Low A finishing on an E.

B – E, B Double Gracenote – C
   1) Play a B.
   2) Do an E gracenote while on B.
   3) Play a C.

B – E, B Double Gracenote – D
   1) Play a B.
   2) Do an E gracenote while on B.
   3) Play a D.

B – E, B Double Gracenote – E
   1) Play a B.
   2) Do an E gracenote while on B.
   3) Play an E.

C – E, B Double Gracenote – C
1) Play a C.
2) Do an E gracenote while on C.
3) Do a Strike to B while still on C.

C – E, B Double Gracenote – D
1) Play a C.
2) Do an E gracenote while on C.
3) Do a Strike to B finishing on a D.

C – E, B Double Gracenote – E
1) Play a C.
2) Do an E gracenote while on C.
3) Do a Strike to B finishing on an E.

D – E, B Double Gracenote – C
1) Play a D.
2) Do an E gracenote while on D.
3) Do a Strike to B finishing on a C.

D – E, B Double Gracenote – D
1) Play a D.
2) Do an E gracenote while on D.
3) Do a Strike to B while still on D.

D – E, B Double Gracenote – E
1) Play a D.
2) Do an E gracenote while on D.
3) Do a Strike to B finishing on an E.

C – E, C Double Gracenote – D
1) Play a C.
2) Do an E gracenote while on C.
3) Play a D.

C – E, C Double Gracenote – E
1) Play a C.
2) Do an E gracenote while on C.
3) Play an E.

D – E, C Double Gracenote – D
1) Play a D.
2) Do an E gracenote while on D.
3) Do a Strike to C while still on D.

D – E, C Double Gracenote – E
1) Play a D.
2) Do an E gracenote while on D.
3) Do a Strike to C finishing on an E.

D – E, D Double Gracenote – E
1) Play a D.
2) Do an E gracenote while on D.
3) Play an E.

The E Double Gracenote is typically played between the first and last note of the embellishment.

F Double Gracenotes

Low G – F, Low G Double Gracenote – Low A

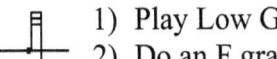
1) Play Low G.
2) Do an F gracenote while on Low G.
3) Play Low A.

Low G – F, Low G Double Gracenote – B
1) Play Low G.
2) Do an F gracenote while on Low G.
3) Play a B.

Low G – F, Low G Double Gracenote – C
1) Play Low G.
2) Do an F gracenote while on Low G.
3) Play a C.

Low G – F, Low G Double Gracenote – D
1) Play Low G.
2) Do an F gracenote while on Low G.
3) Play a D.

Low G – F, Low G Double Gracenote – E
1) Play Low G.
2) Do an F gracenote while on Low G.
3) Play an E.

Low G – F, Low G Double Gracenote – F
 1) Play Low G.
 2) Do an F gracenote while on Low G.
 3) Play an F.

Low A – F, Low G Double Gracenote – Low A
 1) Play Low A.
 2) Do an F gracenote while on Low A.
 3) Do a Strike to Low G while still on Low A.

Low A – F, Low G Double Gracenote – B
 1) Play Low A.
 2) Do an F gracenote while on Low A.
 3) Do a Strike to Low G finishing on a B.

Low A – F, Low G Double Gracenote – C
 1) Play Low A.
 2) Do an F gracenote while on Low A.
 3) Do a Strike to Low G finishing on a C.

Low A – F, Low G Double Gracenote – D
 1) Play Low A.
 2) Do an F gracenote while on Low A.
 3) Do a Strike to Low G finishing on a D.

Low A – F, Low G Double Gracenote – E
 1) Play Low A.
 2) Do an F gracenote while on Low A.
 3) Do a Strike to Low G finishing on an E.

Low A – F, Low G Double Gracenote – F

1) Play Low A.
2) Do an F gracenote while on Low A.
3) Do a Strike to Low G finishing on an F.

B – F, Low G Double Gracenote – Low A

1) Play a B.
2) Do an F gracenote while on B.
3) Do a Strike to Low G finishing on Low A.

B – F, Low G Double Gracenote – B

1) Play a B.
2) Do an F gracenote while on B.
3) Do a Strike to Low G while still on B.

B – F, Low G Double Gracenote – C

1) Play a B.
2) Do an F gracenote while on B.
3) Do a Strike to Low G finishing on C.

B – F, Low G Double Gracenote – D

1) Play a B.
2) Do an F gracenote while on B.
3) Do a Strike to Low G finishing on a D.

B – F, Low G Double Gracenote – E

1) Play a B.
2) Do an F gracenote while on B.
3) Do a Strike to Low G finishing on an E.

B – F, Low G Double Gracenote – F
1) Play a B.
2) Do an F gracenote while on B.
3) Do a Strike to Low G finishing an F.

C – F, Low G Double Gracenote – Low A
1) Play a C.
2) Do an F gracenote while on C.
3) Do a Strike to Low G finishing on Low A.

C – F, Low G Double Gracenote – B
1) Play a C.
2) Do an F gracenote while on C.
3) Do a Strike to Low G finishing on a B.

C – F, Low G Double Gracenote – C
1) Play a C.
2) Do an F gracenote while on C.
3) Do a Strike to Low G while still on C.

C – F, Low G Double Gracenote – D
1) Play a C.
2) Do an F gracenote while on C.
3) Do a Strike to Low G finishing on a D.

C – F, Low G Double Gracenote – E
1) Play a C.
2) Do an F gracenote while on C.
3) Do a Strike to Low G finishing on an E.

C – F, Low G Double Gracenote – F

1) Play a C.
2) Do an F gracenote while on C.
3) Do a Strike to Low G finishing on an F.

D – F, Low G Double Gracenote – Low A

1) Play a D.
2) Do an F gracenote while on D.
3) Do a Strike to Low G finishing on Low A.

D – F, Low G Double Gracenote – B

1) Play a D.
2) Do an F gracenote while on D.
3) Do a Strike to Low G finishing on a B.

D – F, Low G Double Gracenote – C

1) Play a D.
2) Do an F gracenote while on D.
3) Do a Strike to Low G finishing on a C.

D – F, Low G Double Gracenote – D

1) Play a D.
2) Do an F gracenote while on D.
3) Do a Strike to Low G while still on D.

D – F, Low G Double Gracenote – E

1) Play a D.
2) Do an F gracenote while on D.
3) Do a Strike to Low G finishing on an E.

D – F, Low G Double Gracenote – F
1) Play a D.
2) Do an F gracenote while on D.
3) Do a Strike to Low G finishing on an F.

E – F, Low G Double Gracenote – Low A
1) Play an E.
2) Do an F gracenote while on E.
3) Do a Strike to Low G finishing on Low A.

E – F, Low G Double Gracenote – B
1) Play an E.
2) Do an F gracenote while on E.
3) Do a Strike to Low G finishing on a B.

E – F, Low G Double Gracenote – C
1) Play an E.
2) Do an F gracenote while on E.
3) Do a Strike to Low G finishing on a C.

E – F, Low G Double Gracenote – D
1) Play an E.
2) Do an F gracenote while on E.
3) Do a Strike to Low G finishing on a D.

E – F, Low G Double Gracenote – E
1) Play an E.
2) Do an F gracenote while on E.
3) Do a Strike to Low G while still on an E.

E – F, Low G Double Gracenote – F

   1) Play an E.
   2) Do an F gracenote while on E.
   3) Do a Strike to Low G finishing on an F.

Low A – F, Low A Double Gracenote – B

   1) Play Low A.
   2) Do an F gracenote while on Low A.
   3) Play a B.

Low A – F, Low A Double Gracenote – C

   1) Play Low A.
   2) Do an F gracenote while on Low A.
   3) Play a C.

Low A – F, Low A Double Gracenote – D

   1) Play Low A.
   2) Do an F gracenote while on Low A.
   3) Play a D.

Low A – F, Low A Double Gracenote – E

   1) Play Low A.
   2) Do an F gracenote while on Low A.
   3) Play an E.

Low A – F, Low A Double Gracenote – F

   1) Play Low A.
   2) Do an F gracenote while on Low A.
   3) Play an F.

B – F, Low A Double Gracenote – B
1) Play a B.
2) Do an F gracenote while on B.
3) Do a Strike to Low A while still on a B.

B – F, Low A Double Gracenote – C
1) Play a B.
2) Do an F gracenote while on B.
3) Do a Strike to Low A finishing on a C.

B – F, Low A Double Gracenote – D
1) Play a B.
2) Do an F gracenote while on B.
3) Do a Strike to Low A finishing on a D.

B – F, Low A Double Gracenote – E
1) Play a B.
2) Do an F gracenote while on B.
3) Do a Strike to Low A finishing on an E.

B – F, Low A Double Gracenote – F
1) Play a B.
2) Do an F gracenote while on B.
3) Do a Strike to Low A finishing on an F.

C – F, Low A Double Gracenote – B
1) Play a C.
2) Do an F gracenote while on C.
3) Do a Strike to Low A finishing on a B.

C – F, Low A Double Gracenote – C
1) Play a C.
2) Do an F gracenote while on C.
3) Do a Strike to Low A while still on a C.

C – F, Low A Double Gracenote – D
1) Play a C.
2) Do an F gracenote while on C.
3) Do a Strike to Low A finishing on a D.

C – F, Low A Double Gracenote – E
1) Play a C.
2) Do an F gracenote while on C.
3) Do a Strike to Low A finishing on an E.

C – F, Low A Double Gracenote – F
1) Play a C.
2) Do an F gracenote while on C.
3) Do a Strike to Low A finishing on an F.

D – F, Low A Double Gracenote – B
1) Play a D.
2) Do an F gracenote while on D.
3) Do a Strike to Low A finishing on a B.

D – F, Low A Double Gracenote – C
1) Play a D.
2) Do an F gracenote while on D.
3) Do a Strike to Low A finishing on a C.

D – F, Low A Double Gracenote – D
1) Play a D.
2) Do an F gracenote while on D.
3) Do a Strike to Low A while still on a D.

D – F, Low A Double Gracenote – E
1) Play a D.
2) Do an F gracenote while on D.
3) Do a Strike to Low A finishing on an E.

D – F, Low A Double Gracenote – F
1) Play a D.
2) Do an F gracenote while on D.
3) Do a Strike to Low A finishing on an F.

E – F, Low A Double Gracenote – B
1) Play an E.
2) Do an F gracenote while on E.
3) Do a Strike to Low A finishing on a B.

E – F, Low A Double Gracenote – C
1) Play an E.
2) Do an F gracenote while on E.
3) Do a Strike to Low A finishing on a C.

E – F, Low A Double Gracenote – D
1) Play an E.
2) Do an F gracenote while on E.
3) Do a Strike to Low A finishing on a D.

E – F, Low A Double Gracenote – E
   1) Play an E.
   2) Do an F gracenote while on E.
   3) Do a Strike to Low A finishing on an E.

E – F, Low A Double Gracenote – F
   1) Play an E.
   2) Do an F gracenote while on E.
   3) Do a Strike to Low A finishing on an F.

B – F, B Double Gracenote – C
   1) Play a B.
   2) Do an F gracenote while on B.
   3) Play a C.

B – F, B Double Gracenote – D
   1) Play a B.
   2) Do an F gracenote while on B.
   3) Play a D.

B – F, B Double Gracenote – E
   1) Play a B.
   2) Do an F gracenote while on B.
   3) Play an E.

B – F, B Double Gracenote – F
   1) Play a B.
   2) Do an F gracenote while on B.
   3) Play an F.

C – F, B Double Gracenote – C
1) Play a C.
2) Do an F gracenote while on C.
3) Do a Strike to B while still on C.

C – F, B Double Gracenote – D
1) Play a C.
2) Do an F gracenote while on C.
3) Do a Strike to B finishing on a D.

C – F, B Double Gracenote – E
1) Play a C.
2) Do an F gracenote while on C.
3) Do a Strike to B finishing on an E.

C – F, B Double Gracenote – F
1) Play a C.
2) Do an F gracenote while on C.
3) Do a Strike to B finishing on an F.

D – F, B Double Gracenote – C
1) Play a D.
2) Do an F gracenote while on D.
3) Do a Strike to B finishing on a C.

D – F, B Double Gracenote – D
1) Play a D.
2) Do an F gracenote while on D.
3) Do a Strike to B while still on D.

D – F, B Double Gracenote – E

1) Play a D.
2) Do an F gracenote while on D.
3) Do a Strike to B finishing on an E.

D – F, B Double Gracenote – F

1) Play a D.
2) Do an F gracenote while on D.
3) Do a Strike to B finishing on an F.

E – F, B Double Gracenote – C

1) Play an E.
2) Do an F gracenote while on E.
3) Do a Strike to B finishing on a C.

E – F, B Double Gracenote – D

1) Play an E.
2) Do an F gracenote while on E.
3) Do a Strike to B finishing on a D.

E – F, B Double Gracenote – E

1) Play an E.
2) Do an F gracenote while on E.
3) Do a Strike to B while still on an E.

E – F, B Double Gracenote – F

1) Play an E.
2) Do an F gracenote while on E.
3) Do a Strike to B finishing on an F.

C – F, C Double Gracenote – D

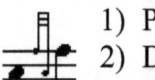
1) Play a C.
2) Do an F gracenote while on C.
3) Play a D.

C – F, C Double Gracenote – E

1) Play a C.
2) Do an F gracenote while on C.
3) Play an E.

C – F, C Double Gracenote – F

1) Play a C.
2) Do an F gracenote while on C.
3) Play an F.

D – F, C Double Gracenote – D

1) Play a D.
2) Do an F gracenote while on D.
3) Do a Strike to C while still on D.

D – F, C Double Gracenote – E

1) Play a D.
2) Do an F gracenote while on D.
3) Do a Strike to C finishing on an E.

D – F, C Double Gracenote – F

1) Play a D.
2) Do an F gracenote while on D.
3) Do a Strike to C finishing on an F.

E – F, C Double Gracenote – D

    1) Play an E.
    2) Do an F gracenote while on E.
    3) Do a Strike to C finishing on D.

E – F, C Double Gracenote – E

    1) Play an E.
    2) Do an F gracenote while on E.
    3) Do a Strike to C while still on an E.

E – F, C Double Gracenote – F

    1) Play an E.
    2) Do an F gracenote while on E.
    3) Do a Strike to C finishing on an F.

D – F, D Double Gracenote – E

    1) Play a D.
    2) Do an F gracenote while on D.
    3) Play an E.

D – F, D Double Gracenote – F

    1) Play a D.
    2) Do an F gracenote while on D.
    3) Play an F.

E – F, D Double Gracenote – E
    1) Play an E.
    2) Do an F gracenote while on E.
    3) Do a Strike to D while still on E.

E – F, D Double Gracenote – F

1) Play an E.
2) Do an F gracenote while on E.
3) Do a Strike to D finishing on an F.

E – F, E Double Gracenote – F

1) Play an E.
2) Do an F gracenote while on E.
3) Play an F.

The F Double Gracenote is typically played between the first and last note of the embellishment.

High G Double Gracenote

Low G – High G, Low G Double Gracenote – Low A

1) Play Low G.
2) Do a G gracenote while on Low G.
3) Play Low A.

Low G – High G, Low G Double Gracenote – B
1) Play Low G.
2) Do a G gracenote while on Low G.
3) Play a B.

Low G – High G, Low G Double Gracenote – C
1) Play Low G.
2) Do a G gracenote while on Low G.
3) Play a C.

Low G – High G, Low G Double Gracenote – D
1) Play Low G.
2) Do a G gracenote while on Low G.
3) Play a D.

Low G – High G, Low G Double Gracenote – E
1) Play Low G.
2) Do a G gracenote while on Low G.
3) Play an E.

Low G – High G, Low G Double Gracenote – F
1) Play Low G.
2) Do a G gracenote while on Low G.
3) Play an F.

Low G – High G, Low G Double Gracenote – High G
1) Play Low G.
2) Do a G gracenote while on Low G.
3) Play High G.

Low A – High G, Low G Double Gracenote – Low A
1) Play Low A.
2) Do a G gracenote while on Low A.
3) Do a Strike to Low G while still on Low A.

Low A – High G, Low G Double Gracenote – B
1) Play Low A.
2) Do a G gracenote while on Low A.
3) Do a Strike to Low G finishing on a B.

Low A – High G, Low G Double Gracenote – C
1) Play Low A.
2) Do a G gracenote while on Low A.
3) Do a Strike to Low G finishing on a C.

Low A – High G, Low G Double Gracenote – D
1) Play Low A.
2) Do a G gracenote while on Low A.
3) Do a Strike to Low G finishing on a D.

Low A – High G, Low G Double Gracenote – E
1) Play Low A.
2) Do a G gracenote while on Low A.
3) Do a Strike to Low G finishing on an E.

Low A – High G, Low G Double Gracenote – F
1) Play Low A.
2) Do a G gracenote while on Low A.
3) Do a Strike to Low G finishing on an F.

Low A – High G, Low G Double Gracenote – High G
  1) Play Low A.
  2) Do a G gracenote while on Low A.
  3) Do a Strike to Low G finishing on High G.

B – High G, Low G Double Gracenote – Low A
  1) Play a B.
  2) Do a G gracenote while on a B.
  3) Do a Strike to Low G finishing on Low A.

B – High G, Low G Double Gracenote – B
  1) Play a B.
  2) Do a G gracenote while on a B.
  3) Do a Strike to Low G while still on a B.

B – High G, Low G Double Gracenote – C
  1) Play a B.
  2) Do a G gracenote while on a B.
  3) Do a Strike to Low G finishing on a C.

B – High G, Low G Double Gracenote – D
  1) Play a B.
  2) Do a G gracenote while on a B.
  3) Do a Strike to Low G finishing on a D.

B – High G, Low G Double Gracenote – E
  1) Play a B.
  2) Do a G gracenote while on a B.
  3) Do a Strike to Low G finishing on an E.

B – High G, Low G Double Gracenote – F
1) Play a B.
2) Do a G gracenote while on a B.
3) Do a Strike to Low G finishing on an F.

B – High G, Low G Double Gracenote – High G
1) Play a B.
2) Do a G gracenote while on a B.
3) Do a Strike to Low G finishing on High G.

C – High G, Low G Double Gracenote – Low A
1) Play a C.
2) Do a G gracenote while on a C.
3) Do a Strike to Low G finishing on Low A.

C – High G, Low G Double Gracenote – B
1) Play a C.
2) Do a G gracenote while on a C.
3) Do a Strike to Low G finishing on a B.

C – High G, Low G Double Gracenote – C
1) Play a C.
2) Do a G gracenote while on a C.
3) Do a Strike to Low G while still on a C.

C – High G, Low G Double Gracenote – D
1) Play a C.
2) Do a G gracenote while on a C.
3) Do a Strike to Low G finishing on a D.

C – High G, Low G Double Gracenote – E
1) Play a C.
2) Do a G gracenote while on a C.
3) Do a Strike to Low G finishing on an E.

C – High G, Low G Double Gracenote – F
1) Play a C.
2) Do a G gracenote while on a C.
3) Do a Strike to Low G finishing on an F.

C – High G, Low G Double Gracenote – High G
1) Play a C.
2) Do a G gracenote while on a C.
3) Do a Strike to Low G finishing on High G.

D – High G, Low G Double Gracenote – Low A
1) Play a D.
2) Do a G gracenote while on a D.
3) Do a Strike to Low G finishing on Low A.

D – High G, Low G Double Gracenote – B
1) Play a D.
2) Do a G gracenote while on a D.
3) Do a Strike to Low G finishing on a B.

D – High G, Low G Double Gracenote – C
1) Play a D.
2) Do a G gracenote while on a D.
3) Do a Strike to Low G finishing on a C.

D – High G, Low G Double Gracenote – D
  1) Play a D.
  2) Do a G gracenote while on a D.
  3) Do a Strike to Low G while still on D.

D – High G, Low G Double Gracenote – E
  1) Play a D.
  2) Do a G gracenote while on a D.
  3) Do a Strike to Low G finishing on an E.

D – High G, Low G Double Gracenote – F
  1) Play a D.
  2) Do a G gracenote while on a D.
  3) Do a Strike to Low G finishing on an F.

D – High G, Low G Double Gracenote – High G
  1) Play a D.
  2) Do a G gracenote while on a D.
  3) Do a Strike to Low G while still on High G.

E – High G, Low G Double Gracenote – Low A
  1) Play an E.
  2) Do a G gracenote while on an E.
  3) Do a Strike to Low G finishing on Low A.

E – High G, Low G Double Gracenote – B
  1) Play an E.
  2) Do a G gracenote while on an E.
  3) Do a Strike to Low G finishing on a B.

E – High G, Low G Double Gracenote – C
 1) Play an E.
 2) Do a G gracenote while on an E.
 3) Do a Strike to Low G finishing on a C.

E – High G, Low G Double Gracenote – D
 1) Play an E.
 2) Do a G gracenote while on an E.
 3) Do a Strike to Low G finishing on a D.

E – High G, Low G Double Gracenote – E
 1) Play an E.
 2) Do a G gracenote while on an E.
 3) Do a Strike to Low G while still on an E.

E – High G, Low G Double Gracenote – F
 1) Play an E.
 2) Do a G gracenote while on an E.
 3) Do a Strike to Low G finishing on an F.

E – High G, Low G Double Gracenote – High G
 1) Play an E.
 2) Do a G gracenote while on an E.
 3) Do a Strike to Low G finishing on High G.

F – High G, Low G Double Gracenote – Low A
 1) Play an F.
 2) Do a G gracenote while on an F.
 3) Do a Strike to Low G finishing on Low A.

F – High G, Low G Double Gracenote – B
1) Play an F.
2) Do a G gracenote while on an F.
3) Do a Strike to Low G finishing on a B.

F – High G, Low G Double Gracenote – C
1) Play an F.
2) Do a G gracenote while on an F.
3) Do a Strike to Low G finishing on a C.

F – High G, Low G Double Gracenote – D
1) Play an F.
2) Do a G gracenote while on an F.
3) Do a Strike to Low G finishing on a D.

F – High G, Low G Double Gracenote – E
1) Play an F.
2) Do a G gracenote while on an F.
3) Do a Strike to Low G finishing on an E.

F – High G, Low G Double Gracenote – F
1) Play an F.
2) Do a G gracenote while on an F.
3) Do a Strike to Low G while still on an F.

F – High G, Low G Double Gracenote – High G
1) Play an F.
2) Do a G gracenote while on an F.
3) Do a Strike to Low G finishing on High G.

Low A – High G, Low A Double Gracenote – B
1) Play Low A.
2) Do a G gracenote while on Low A.
3) Play a B.

Low A – High G, Low A Double Gracenote – C
1) Play Low A.
2) Do a G gracenote while on Low A.
3) Play a C.

Low A – High G, Low A Double Gracenote – D
1) Play Low A.
2) Do a G gracenote while on Low A.
3) Play a D.

Low A – High G, Low A Double Gracenote – E
1) Play Low A.
2) Do a G gracenote while on Low A.
3) Play an E.

Low A – High G, Low A Double Gracenote – F
1) Play Low A.
2) Do a G gracenote while on Low A.
3) Play an F.

Low A – High G, Low A Double Gracenote – High G
1) Play Low A.
2) Do a G gracenote while on Low A.
3) Play High G.

B – High G, Low A Double Gracenote – B
1) Play a B.
2) Do a G gracenote while on a B.
3) Do a Strike to Low A while still on a B.

B – High G, Low A Double Gracenote – C
1) Play a B.
2) Do a G gracenote while on a B.
3) Do a Strike to Low A finishing on a C.

B – High G, Low A Double Gracenote – D
1) Play a B.
2) Do a G gracenote while on a B.
3) Do a Strike to Low A finishing on a D.

B – High G, Low A Double Gracenote – E
1) Play a B.
2) Do a G gracenote while on a B.
3) Do a Strike to Low A finishing on an E.

B – High G, Low A Double Gracenote – F
1) Play a B.
2) Do a G gracenote while on a B.
3) Do a Strike to Low A finishing on an F.

B – High G, Low A Double Gracenote – High G
1) Play a B.
2) Do a G gracenote while on a B.
3) Do a Strike to Low A finishing on High G.

C – High G, Low A Double Gracenote – B
1) Play a C.
2) Do a G gracenote while on a C.
3) Do a Strike to Low A finishing on a B.

C – High G, Low A Double Gracenote – C
1) Play a C.
2) Do a G gracenote while on a C.
3) Do a Strike to Low A while still on a C.

C – High G, Low A Double Gracenote – D
1) Play a C.
2) Do a G gracenote while on a C.
3) Do a Strike to Low A finishing on a D.

C – High G, Low A Double Gracenote – E
1) Play a C.
2) Do a G gracenote while on a C.
3) Do a Strike to Low A finishing on an E.

C – High G, Low A Double Gracenote – F
1) Play a C.
2) Do a G gracenote while on a C.
3) Do a Strike to Low A finishing on an F.

C – High G, Low A Double Gracenote – High G
1) Play a C.
2) Do a G gracenote while on a C.
3) Do a Strike to Low A while still on High G.

D – High G, Low A Double Gracenote – B
1) Play a D.
2) Do a G gracenote while on a D.
3) Do a Strike to Low A finishing on a B.

D – High G, Low A Double Gracenote – C
1) Play a D.
2) Do a G gracenote while on a D.
3) Do a Strike to Low A finishing on a C.

D – High G, Low A Double Gracenote – D
1) Play a D.
2) Do a G gracenote while on a D.
3) Do a Strike to Low A while still on a D.

D – High G, Low A Double Gracenote – E
1) Play a D.
2) Do a G gracenote while on a D.
3) Do a Strike to Low A finishing on an E.

D – High G, Low A Double Gracenote – F
1) Play a D.
2) Do a G gracenote while on a D.
3) Do a Strike to Low A finishing on an F.

D – High G, Low A Double Gracenote – High G
1) Play a D.
2) Do a G gracenote while on a D.
3) Do a Strike to Low A while still on High G.

E – High G, Low A Double Gracenote – B
1) Play an E.
2) Do a G gracenote while on an E.
3) Do a Strike to Low A finishing on a B.

E – High G, Low A Double Gracenote – C
1) Play an E.
2) Do a G gracenote while on an E.
3) Do a Strike to Low A finishing on a C.

E – High G, Low A Double Gracenote – D
1) Play an E.
2) Do a G gracenote while on an E.
3) Do a Strike to Low A finishing on a D.

E – High G, Low A Double Gracenote – E
1) Play an E.
2) Do a G gracenote while on an E.
3) Do a Strike to Low A while still on an E.

E – High G, Low A Double Gracenote – F
1) Play an E.
2) Do a G gracenote while on an E.
3) Do a Strike to Low A finishing on an F.

E – High G, Low A Double Gracenote – High G
1) Play an E.
2) Do a G gracenote while on an E.
3) Do a Strike to Low A finishing on High G.

F – High G, Low A Double Gracenote – B

1) Play an F.
2) Do a G gracenote while on an F.
3) Do a Strike to Low A finishing on a B.

F – High G, Low A Double Gracenote – C

1) Play an F.
2) Do a G gracenote while on an F.
3) Do a Strike to Low A finishing on a C.

F – High G, Low A Double Gracenote – D

1) Play an F.
2) Do a G gracenote while on an F.
3) Do a Strike to Low A finishing on a D.

F – High G, Low A Double Gracenote – E

1) Play an F.
2) Do a G gracenote while on an F.
3) Do a Strike to Low A finishing on an E.

F – High G, Low A Double Gracenote – F

1) Play an F.
2) Do a G gracenote while on an F.
3) Do a Strike to Low A while still on an F.

F – High G, Low A Double Gracenote – High G

1) Play an F.
2) Do a G gracenote while on an F.
3) Do a Strike to Low A finishing on High G.

B – High G, B Double Gracenote – C
　　1) Play a B.
　　2) Do a G gracenote while on a B.
　　3) Play a C.

B – High G, B Double Gracenote – D
　　1) Play a B.
　　2) Do a G gracenote while on a B.
　　3) Play a D.

B – High G, B Double Gracenote – E
　　1) Play a B.
　　2) Do a G gracenote while on a B.
　　3) Play an E.

B – High G, B Double Gracenote – F
　　1) Play a B.
　　2) Do a G gracenote while on a B.
　　3) Play an F.

B – High G, B Double Gracenote – High G
　　1) Play a B.
　　2) Do a G gracenote while on a B.
　　3) Play High G.

C – High G, B Double Gracenote – C
　　1) Play a C.
　　2) Do a G gracenote while on a C.
　　3) Do a Strike to B while still on a C.

C – High G, B Double Gracenote – D
1) Play a C.
2) Do a G gracenote while on a C.
3) Do a Strike to B finishing on a D.

C – High G, B Double Gracenote – E
1) Play a C.
2) Do a G gracenote while on a C.
3) Do a Strike to B finishing on an E.

C – High G, B Double Gracenote – F
1) Play a C.
2) Do a G gracenote while on a C.
3) Do a Strike to B finishing on an F.

C – High G, B Double Gracenote – High G
1) Play a C.
2) Do a G gracenote while on a C.
3) Do a Strike to B finishing on High G.

D – High G, B Double Gracenote – C
1) Play a D.
2) Do a G gracenote while on a D.
3) Do a Strike to B finishing on a C.

D – High G, B Double Gracenote – D
1) Play a D.
2) Do a G gracenote while on a D.
3) Do a Strike to B while still on a D.

D – High G, B Double Gracenote – E
1) Play a D.
2) Do a G gracenote while on a D.
3) Do a Strike to B finishing on an E.

D – High G, B Double Gracenote – F
1) Play a D.
2) Do a G gracenote while on a D.
3) Do a Strike to B finishing on an F.

D – High G, B Double Gracenote – High G
1) Play a D.
2) Do a G gracenote while on a D.
3) Do a Strike to B finishing on High G.

D – High G, B Double Gracenote – C
1) Play a D.
2) Do a G gracenote while on a D.
3) Do a Strike to B finishing on a C.

D – High G, B Double Gracenote – D
1) Play a D.
2) Do a G gracenote while on a D.
3) Do a Strike to B while still on a D.

D – High G, B Double Gracenote – E
1) Play a D.
2) Do a G gracenote while on a D.
3) Do a Strike to B finishing on an E.

D – High G, B Double Gracenote – F
1) Play a D.
2) Do a G gracenote while on a D.
3) Do a Strike to B finishing on an F.

D – High G, B Double Gracenote – High G
1) Play a D.
2) Do a G gracenote while on a D.
3) Do a Strike to B finishing on High G.

E – High G, B Double Gracenote – C
1) Play an E.
2) Do a G gracenote while on an E.
3) Do a Strike to B finishing on a C.

E – High G, B Double Gracenote – D
1) Play an E.
2) Do a G gracenote while on an E.
3) Do a Strike to B finishing on a D.

E – High G, B Double Gracenote – E
1) Play an E.
2) Do a G gracenote while on an E.
3) Do a Strike to B while still on an E.

E – High G, B Double Gracenote – F
1) Play an E.
2) Do a G gracenote while on an E.
3) Do a Strike to B finishing on an F.

E – High G, B Double Gracenote – High G
1) Play an E.
2) Do a G gracenote while on an E.
3) Do a Strike to B finishing on High G.

F – High G, B Double Gracenote – C
1) Play an F.
2) Do a G gracenote while on an F.
3) Do a Strike to B finishing on a C.

F – High G, B Double Gracenote – D
1) Play an F.
2) Do a G gracenote while on an F.
3) Do a Strike to B finishing on a D.

F – High G, B Double Gracenote – E
1) Play an F.
2) Do a G gracenote while on an F.
3) Do a Strike to B finishing on an E.

F – High G, B Double Gracenote – F
1) Play an F.
2) Do a G gracenote while on an F.
3) Do a Strike to B while still on an F.

F – High G, B Double Gracenote – High G
1) Play an F.
2) Do a G gracenote while on High G.
3) Do a Strike to B finishing on High G.

C – High G, C Double Gracenote – D
1) Play a C.
2) Do a G gracenote while on a C.
3) Play a D.

C – High G, C Double Gracenote – E
1) Play a C.
2) Do a G gracenote while on a C.
3) Play an E.

C – High G, C Double Gracenote – F
1) Play a C.
2) Do a G gracenote while on a C.
3) Play an F.

C – High G, C Double Gracenote – High G
1) Play a C.
2) Do a G gracenote while on a C.
3) Play High G.

D – High G, C Double Gracenote – D
1) Play a D.
2) Do a G gracenote while on a D.
3) Do a Strike to C while still on a D.

D – High G, C Double Gracenote – E
1) Play a D.
2) Do a G gracenote while on a D.
3) Do a Strike to C finishing on an E.

D – High G, C Double Gracenote – F

1) Play a D.
2) Do a G gracenote while on a D.
3) Do a Strike to C finishing on an F.

D – High G, C Double Gracenote – High G

1) Play a D.
2) Do a G gracenote while on a D.
3) Do a Strike to C finishing on High G.

E – High G, C Double Gracenote – D

1) Play an E.
2) Do a G gracenote while on an E.
3) Do a Strike to C finishing on a D.

E – High G, C Double Gracenote – E

1) Play an E.
2) Do a G gracenote while on an E.
3) Do a Strike to C while still on an E.

E – High G, C Double Gracenote – F

1) Play an E.
2) Do a G gracenote while on an E.
3) Do a Strike to C finishing on an F.

E – High G, C Double Gracenote – High G

1) Play an E.
2) Do a G gracenote while on an E.
3) Do a Strike to C finishing on High G.

F – High G, C Double Gracenote – D
1) Play an F.
2) Do a G gracenote while on an F.
3) Do a Strike to C finishing on a D.

F – High G, C Double Gracenote – E
1) Play an F.
2) Do a G gracenote while on an F.
3) Do a Strike to C finishing on an E.

F – High G, C Double Gracenote – F
1) Play an F.
2) Do a G gracenote while on an F.
3) Do a Strike to C while still on an F.

F – High G, C Double Gracenote – High G
1) Play an F.
2) Do a G gracenote while on an F.
3) Do a Strike to C finishing on High G.

D – High G, D Double Gracenote – E
1) Play a D.
2) Do a G gracenote while on a D.
3) Play an E.

D – High G, D Double Gracenote – F
1) Play a D.
2) Do a G gracenote while on a D.
3) Play an F.

D – High G, D Double Gracenote – High G
1) Play a D.
2) Do a G gracenote while on a D.
3) Play High G.

E – High G, D Double Gracenote – E
1) Play an E.
2) Do a G gracenote while on a E.
3) Do a Strike to D while still on an E.

E – High G, D Double Gracenote – F
1) Play an E.
2) Do a G gracenote while on a E.
3) Do a Strike to D finishing on an F.

E – High G, D Double Gracenote – High G
1) Play an E.
2) Do a G gracenote while on a E.
3) Do a Strike to D finishing on High G.

F – High G, D Double Gracenote – E
1) Play an F.
2) Do a G gracenote while on a F.
3) Do a Strike to D finishing on an E.

F – High G, D Double Gracenote – F
1) Play an F.
2) Do a G gracenote while on an F.
3) Do a Strike to D while still on an F.

F – High G, D Double Gracenote – High G

    1) Play an F.
    2) Do a G gracenote while on an F.
    3) Do a Strike to D finishing on High G.

E – High G, E Double Gracenote – F

    1) Play an E.
    2) Do a G gracenote while on an E.
    3) Play an F.

E – High G, E Double Gracenote – High G

    1) Play an E.
    2) Do a G gracenote while on an E.
    3) Play High G.

F – High G, E Double Gracenote – F

    1) Play an F.
    2) Do a G gracenote while on an F.
    3) Do a Strike to E while still on an F.

F – High G, E Double Gracenote – High G

    1) Play an F.
    2) Do a G gracenote while on an F.
    3) Do a Strike to E finishing on High G.

F – High G, F Double Gracenote – High G

    1) Play an F.
    2) Do a G gracenote while on an F.
    3) Play High G.

The High G Double Gracenote is typically played between the first and last note of the embellishment.

High A Double Gracenote

Low G – High A, Low G Double Gracenote – Low A
1) Play Low G.
2) Play High A.
3) Play Low G again.
4) Play Low A.

Low G – High A, Low G Double Gracenote – B
1) Play Low G.
2) Play High A.
3) Play Low G again.
4) Play a B.

Low G – High A, Low G Double Gracenote – C
1) Play Low G.
2) Play High A.
3) Play Low G again.
4) Play a C.

Low G – High A, Low G Double Gracenote – D
1) Play Low G.
2) Play High A.
3) Play Low G again.
4) Play a D.

Low G – High A, Low G Double Gracenote – E
1) Play Low G.
2) Play High A.
3) Play Low G again.
4) Play an E.

Low G – High A, Low G Double Gracenote – F
1) Play Low G.
2) Play High A.
3) Play Low G again.
4) Play an F.

Low G – High A, Low G Double Gracenote – High G
1) Play Low G.
2) Play High A.
3) Play Low G again.
4) Play High G.

Low G – High A, Low G Double Gracenote – High A
1) Play Low G.
2) Play High A.
3) Play Low G again.
4) Play High A again.

Low A – High A, Low G Double Gracenote – Low A
1) Play Low A.
2) Play High A.
3) Do a Strike to Low G finishing on Low A.

Low A – High A, Low G Double Gracenote – B
1) Play Low A.
2) Play High A.
3) Do a Strike to Low G finishing on a B.

Low A – High A, Low G Double Gracenote – C
1) Play Low A.
2) Play High A.
3) Do a Strike to Low G finishing on a C.

Low A – High A, Low G Double Gracenote – D
1) Play Low A.
2) Play High A.
3) Do a Strike to Low G finishing on a D.

Low A – High A, Low G Double Gracenote – E
1) Play Low A.
2) Play High A.
3) Do a Strike to Low G finishing on an E.

Low A – High A, Low G Double Gracenote – F
1) Play Low A.
2) Play High A.
3) Do a Strike to Low G finishing on an F.

Low A – High A, Low G Double Gracenote – High G
1) Play Low A.
2) Play High A.
3) Do a Strike to Low G finishing on High G.

Low A – High A, Low G Double Gracenote – High A

1) Play Low A.
2) Play High A.
3) Do a Strike to Low G finishing on High A.

B – High A, Low G Double Gracenote – Low A

1) Play a B.
2) Play High A.
3) Do a Strike to Low G finishing on Low A.

B – High A, Low G Double Gracenote – B

1) Play a B.
2) Play High A.
3) Do a Strike to Low G finishing on a B.

B – High A, Low G Double Gracenote – C

1) Play a B.
2) Play High A.
3) Do a Strike to Low G finishing on a C.

B – High A, Low G Double Gracenote – D

1) Play a B.
2) Play High A.
3) Do a Strike to Low G finishing on a D.

B – High A, Low G Double Gracenote – E

1) Play a B.
2) Play High A.
3) Do a Strike to Low G finishing on an E.

B – High A, Low G Double Gracenote – F

1) Play a B.
2) Play High A.
3) Do a Strike to Low G finishing on an F.

B – High A, Low G Double Gracenote – High G

1) Play a B.
2) Play High A.
3) Do a Strike to Low G finishing on High G.

B – High A, Low G Double Gracenote – High A

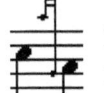
1) Play a B.
2) Play High A.
3) Do a Strike to Low G finishing on High A.

C – High A, Low G Double Gracenote – Low A

1) Play a C.
2) Play High A.
3) Do a Strike to Low G finishing on High A.

C – High A, Low G Double Gracenote – B

1) Play a C.
2) Play High A.
3) Do a Strike to Low G finishing on a B.

C – High A, Low G Double Gracenote – C

1) Play a C.
2) Play High A.
3) Do a Strike to Low G finishing on a C.

C – High A, Low G Double Gracenote – D
1) Play a C.
2) Play High A.
3) Do a Strike to Low G finishing on a D.

C – High A, Low G Double Gracenote – E
1) Play a C.
2) Play High A.
3) Do a Strike to Low G finishing on an E.

C – High A, Low G Double Gracenote – F
1) Play a C.
2) Play High A.
3) Do a Strike to Low G finishing on an F.

C – High A, Low G Double Gracenote – High G
1) Play a C.
2) Play High A.
3) Do a Strike to Low G finishing on High G.

C – High A, Low G Double Gracenote – High A
1) Play a C.
2) Play High A.
3) Do a Strike to Low G finishing on High A.

D – High A, Low G Double Gracenote – Low A
1) Play a D.
2) Play High A.
3) Do a Strike to Low G finishing on Low A.

D – High A, Low G Double Gracenote – B
1) Play a D.
2) Play High A.
3) Do a Strike to Low G finishing on a B.

D – High A, Low G Double Gracenote – C
1) Play a D.
2) Play High A.
3) Do a Strike to Low G finishing on a C.

D – High A, Low G Double Gracenote – D
1) Play a D.
2) Play High A.
3) Do a Strike to Low G finishing on a D.

D – High A, Low G Double Gracenote – E
1) Play a D.
2) Play High A.
3) Do a Strike to Low G finishing on an E.

D – High A, Low G Double Gracenote – F
1) Play a D.
2) Play High A.
3) Do a Strike to Low G finishing on an F.

D – High A, Low G Double Gracenote – High G
1) Play a D.
2) Play High A.
3) Do a Strike to Low G finishing on High G.

D – High A, Low G Double Gracenote – High A
1) Play a D.
2) Play High A.
3) Do a Strike to Low G finishing on High A.

E – High A, Low G Double Gracenote – Low A
1) Play an E.
2) Play High A.
3) Do a Strike to Low G finishing on Low A.

E – High A, Low G Double Gracenote – B
1) Play an E.
2) Play High A.
3) Do a Strike to Low G finishing on a B.

E – High A, Low G Double Gracenote – C
1) Play an E.
2) Play High A.
3) Do a Strike to Low G finishing on a C.

E – High A, Low G Double Gracenote – D
1) Play an E.
2) Play High A.
3) Do a Strike to Low G finishing on a D.

E – High A, Low G Double Gracenote – E
1) Play an E.
2) Play High A.
3) Do a Strike to Low G finishing on an E.

E – High A, Low G Double Gracenote – F
1) Play an E.
2) Play High A.
3) Do a Strike to Low G finishing on an F.

E – High A, Low G Double Gracenote – High G
1) Play an E.
2) Play High A.
3) Do a Strike to Low G finishing on High G.

E – High A, Low G Double Gracenote – High A
1) Play an E.
2) Play High A.
3) Do a Strike to Low G finishing on High A.

F – High A, Low G Double Gracenote – Low A
1) Play an F.
2) Play High A.
3) Do a Strike to Low G finishing on Low A.

F – High A, Low G Double Gracenote – B
1) Play an F.
2) Play High A.
3) Do a Strike to Low G finishing on a B.

F – High A, Low G Double Gracenote – C
1) Play an F.
2) Play High A.
3) Do a Strike to Low G finishing on a C.

F – High A, Low G Double Gracenote – D
1) Play an F.
2) Play High A.
3) Do a Strike to Low G finishing on a D.

F – High A, Low G Double Gracenote – E
1) Play an F.
2) Play High A.
3) Do a Strike to Low G finishing on an E.

F – High A, Low G Double Gracenote – F
1) Play an F.
2) Play High A.
3) Do a Strike to Low G finishing on an F.

F – High A, Low G Double Gracenote – High G
1) Play an F.
2) Play High A.
3) Do a Strike to Low G finishing on High G.

F – High A, Low G Double Gracenote – High A
1) Play an F.
2) Play High A.
3) Do a Strike to Low G finishing on High A.

High G – High A, Low G Double Gracenote – Low A
1) Play High G.
2) Play High A.
3) Do a Strike to Low G finishing on Low A.

High G – High A, Low G Double Gracenote – B
1) Play High G.
2) Play High A.
3) Do a Strike to Low G finishing on a B.

High G – High A, Low G Double Gracenote – C
1) Play High G.
2) Play High A.
3) Do a Strike to Low G finishing on a C.

High G – High A, Low G Double Gracenote – D
1) Play High G.
2) Play High A.
3) Do a Strike to Low G finishing on a D.

High G – High A, Low G Double Gracenote – E
1) Play High G.
2) Play High A.
3) Do a Strike to Low G finishing on an E.

High G – High A, Low G Double Gracenote – F
1) Play High G.
2) Play High A.
3) Do a Strike to Low G finishing on an F.

High G – High A, Low G Double Gracenote – High G
1) Play High G.
2) Play High A.
3) Do a Strike to Low G finishing on High G.

High G – High A, Low G Double Gracenote – High A
1) Play High G.
2) Play High A.
3) Do a Strike to Low G finishing on High A.

Low A – High A, Low A Double Gracenote – B
1) Play Low A.
2) Play High A.
3) Play Low A again.
4) Play a B.

Low A – High A, Low A Double Gracenote – C
1) Play Low A.
2) Play High A.
3) Play Low A again.
4) Play a C.

Low A – High A, Low A Double Gracenote – D
1) Play Low A.
2) Play High A.
3) Play Low A again.
4) Play a D.

Low A – High A, Low A Double Gracenote – E
1) Play Low A.
2) Play High A.
3) Play Low A again.
4) Play an E.

Low A – High A, Low A Double Gracenote – F
1) Play Low A.
2) Play High A.
3) Play Low A again.
4) Play an F.

Low A – High A, Low A Double Gracenote – High G

1) Play Low A.
2) Play High A.
3) Play Low A again.
4) Play High G.

Low A – High A, Low A Double Gracenote – High A

1) Play Low A.
2) Play High A.
3) Play Low A again.
4) Play High A.

B – High A, Low A Double Gracenote – B

1) Play a B.
2) Play High A.
3) Do a Strike to Low A finishing on a B.

B – High A, Low A Double Gracenote – C

4) Play a B.
5) Play High A.
6) Do a Strike to Low A finishing on a C.

B – High A, Low A Double Gracenote – D

1) Play a B.
2) Play High A.
3) Do a Strike to Low A finishing on a D.

B – High A, Low A Double Gracenote – E

1) Play a B.
2) Play High A.
3) Do a Strike to Low A finishing on an E.

B – High A, Low A Double Gracenote – F
1) Play a B.
2) Play High A.
3) Do a Strike to Low A finishing on an F.

B – High A, Low A Double Gracenote – High G
1) Play a B.
2) Play High A.
3) Do a Strike to Low A finishing on High G.

B – High A, Low A Double Gracenote – High A
1) Play a B.
2) Play High A.
3) Do a Strike to Low A finishing on High A.

C – High A, Low A Double Gracenote – B
1) Play a C.
2) Play High A.
3) Do a Strike to Low A finishing on a B.

C – High A, Low A Double Gracenote – C
1) Play a C.
2) Play High A.
3) Do a Strike to Low A finishing on a C.

C – High A, Low A Double Gracenote – D
1) Play a C.
2) Play High A.
3) Do a Strike to Low A finishing on a D.

C – High A, Low A Double Gracenote – E
1) Play a C.
2) Play High A.
3) Do a Strike to Low A finishing on an E.

C – High A, Low A Double Gracenote – F
1) Play a C.
2) Play High A.
3) Do a Strike to Low A finishing on an F.

C – High A, Low A Double Gracenote – High G
1) Play a C.
2) Play High A.
3) Do a Strike to Low A finishing on High G.

C – High A, Low A Double Gracenote – High A
1) Play a C.
2) Play High A.
3) Do a Strike to Low A finishing on High A.

D – High A, Low A Double Gracenote – B
1) Play a D.
2) Play High A.
3) Do a Strike to Low A finishing on a B.

D – High A, Low A Double Gracenote – C
1) Play a D.
2) Play High A.
3) Do a Strike to Low A finishing on a C.

D – High A, Low A Double Gracenote – D
1) Play a D.
2) Play High A.
3) Do a Strike to Low A finishing on a D.

D – High A, Low A Double Gracenote – E
1) Play a D.
2) Play High A.
3) Do a Strike to Low A finishing on an E.

D – High A, Low A Double Gracenote – F
1) Play a D.
2) Play High A.
3) Do a Strike to Low A finishing on an F.

D – High A, Low A Double Gracenote – High G
1) Play a D.
2) Play High A.
3) Do a Strike to Low A finishing on High G.

D – High A, Low A Double Gracenote – High A
1) Play a D.
2) Play High A.
3) Do a Strike to Low A finishing on High A.

E – High A, Low A Double Gracenote – B
1) Play an E.
2) Play High A.
3) Do a Strike to Low A finishing on a B.

E – High A, Low A Double Gracenote – C
1) Play an E.
2) Play High A.
3) Do a Strike to Low A finishing on a C.

E – High A, Low A Double Gracenote – D
1) Play an E.
2) Play High A.
3) Do a Strike to Low A finishing on a D.

E – High A, Low A Double Gracenote – E
1) Play an E.
2) Play High A.
3) Do a Strike to Low A finishing on an E.

E – High A, Low A Double Gracenote – F
1) Play an E.
2) Play High A.
3) Do a Strike to Low A finishing on an F.

E – High A, Low A Double Gracenote – High G
1) Play an E.
2) Play High A.
3) Do a Strike to Low A finishing on High G.

E – High A, Low A Double Gracenote – High A
1) Play an E.
2) Play High A.
3) Do a Strike to Low A finishing on High A.

F – High A, Low A Double Gracenote – B
1) Play an F.
2) Play High A.
3) Do a Strike to Low A finishing on a B.

F – High A, Low A Double Gracenote – C
1) Play an F.
2) Play High A.
3) Do a Strike to Low A finishing on a C.

F – High A, Low A Double Gracenote – D
1) Play an F.
2) Play High A.
3) Do a Strike to Low A finishing on a D.

F – High A, Low A Double Gracenote – E
1) Play an F.
2) Play High A.
3) Do a Strike to Low A finishing on an E.

F – High A, Low A Double Gracenote – F
1) Play an F.
2) Play High A.
3) Do a Strike to Low A finishing on an F.

F – High A, Low A Double Gracenote – High G
1) Play an F.
2) Play High A.
3) Do a Strike to Low A finishing on High G.

F – High A, Low A Double Gracenote – High A
1) Play an F.
2) Play High A.
3) Do a Strike to Low A finishing on High A.

High G – High A, Low A Double Gracenote – B
1) Play High G.
2) Play High A.
3) Do a Strike to Low A finishing on a B.

High G – High A, Low A Double Gracenote – C
1) Play High G.
2) Play High A.
3) Do a Strike to Low A finishing on a C.

High G – High A, Low A Double Gracenote – D
1) Play High G.
2) Play High A.
3) Do a Strike to Low A finishing on a D.

High G – High A, Low A Double Gracenote – E
1) Play High G.
2) Play High A.
3) Do a Strike to Low A finishing on an E.

High G – High A, Low A Double Gracenote – F
1) Play High G.
2) Play High A.
3) Do a Strike to Low A finishing on an F.

High G – High A, Low A Double Gracenote – High G
1) Play High G.
2) Play High A.
3) Do a Strike to Low A finishing on High G.

High G – High A, Low A Double Gracenote – High A
1) Play High G.
2) Play High A.
3) Do a Strike to Low A finishing on High A.

B – High A, B Double Gracenote – C
1) Play a B.
2) Play High A.
3) Play a B again.
4) Play a C.

B – High A, B Double Gracenote – D
1) Play a B.
2) Play High A.
3) Play a B again.
4) Play a D.

B – High A, B Double Gracenote – E
1) Play a B.
2) Play High A.
3) Play a B again.
4) Play an E.

B – High A, B Double Gracenote – F
1) Play a B.
2) Play High A.
3) Play a B again.
4) Play an F.

B – High A, B Double Gracenote – High G

1) Play a B.
2) Play High A.
3) Play a B again.
4) Play High G.

B – High A, B Double Gracenote – High A

1) Play a B.
2) Play High A.
3) Play a B again.
4) Play High A.

C – High A, B Double Gracenote – C

1) Play a C.
2) Play High A.
3) Do a Strike to B finishing on a C.

C – High A, B Double Gracenote – D

1) Play a C.
2) Play High A.
3) Do a Strike to B finishing on a D.

C – High A, B Double Gracenote – E

1) Play a C.
2) Play High A.
3) Do a Strike to B finishing on an E.

C – High A, B Double Gracenote – F

1) Play a C.
2) Play High A.
3) Do a Strike to B finishing on an F.

C – High A, B Double Gracenote – High G
1) Play a C.
2) Play High A.
3) Do a Strike to B finishing on High G.

C – High A, B Double Gracenote – High A
1) Play a C.
2) Play High A.
3) Do a Strike to B finishing on High A.

D – High A, B Double Gracenote – C
1) Play a D.
2) Play High A.
3) Do a Strike to B finishing on a C.

D – High A, B Double Gracenote – D
1) Play a D.
2) Play High A.
3) Do a Strike to B finishing on a D.

D – High A, B Double Gracenote – E
1) Play a D.
2) Play High A.
3) Do a Strike to B finishing on an E.

D – High A, B Double Gracenote – F
1) Play a D.
2) Play High A.
3) Do a Strike to B finishing on an F.

D – High A, B Double Gracenote – High G

1) Play a D.
2) Play High A.
3) Do a Strike to B finishing on High G.

D – High A, B Double Gracenote – High A

1) Play a D.
2) Play High A.
3) Do a Strike to B finishing on High A.

E – High A, B Double Gracenote – C

1) Play an E.
2) Play High A.
3) Do a Strike to B finishing on a C.

E – High A, B Double Gracenote – D

1) Play an E.
2) Play High A.
3) Do a Strike to B finishing on a D.

E – High A, B Double Gracenote – E

1) Play an E.
2) Play High A.
3) Do a Strike to B finishing on an E.

E – High A, B Double Gracenote – F

1) Play an E.
2) Play High A.
3) Do a Strike to B finishing on an F.

E – High A, B Double Gracenote – High G

1) Play an E.
2) Play High A.
3) Do a Strike to B finishing on High G.

E – High A, B Double Gracenote – High A

1) Play an E.
2) Play High A.
3) Do a Strike to B finishing on High A.

F – High A, B Double Gracenote – C

1) Play an F.
2) Play High A.
3) Do a Strike to B finishing on a C.

F – High A, B Double Gracenote – D

1) Play an F.
2) Play High A.
3) Do a Strike to B finishing on a D.

F – High A, B Double Gracenote – E

1) Play an F.
2) Play High A.
3) Do a Strike to B finishing on an E.

F – High A, B Double Gracenote – F

1) Play an F.
2) Play High A.
3) Do a Strike to B finishing on an F.

F – High A, B Double Gracenote – High G
1) Play an F.
2) Play High A.
3) Do a Strike to B finishing on High G.

F – High A, B Double Gracenote – High A
1) Play an F.
2) Play High A.
3) Do a Strike to B finishing on High A.

High G – High A, B Double Gracenote – C
1) Play High G.
2) Play High A.
3) Do a Strike to B finishing on a C.

High G – High A, B Double Gracenote – D
1) Play High G.
2) Play High A.
3) Do a Strike to B finishing on a D.

High G – High A, B Double Gracenote – E
1) Play High G.
2) Play High A.
3) Do a Strike to B finishing on an E.

High G – High A, B Double Gracenote – F
1) Play High G.
2) Play High A.
3) Do a Strike to B finishing on an F.

High G – High A, B Double Gracenote – High G

1) Play High G.
2) Play High A.
3) Do a Strike to B finishing on High G.

High G – High A, B Double Gracenote – High A

1) Play High G.
2) Play High A.
3) Do a Strike to B finishing on High A.

C – High A, C Double Gracenote – D

1) Play a C.
2) Play High A.
3) Play a C again.
4) Play a D.

C – High A, C Double Gracenote – E

1) Play a C.
2) Play High A.
3) Play a C again.
4) Play an E.

C – High A, C Double Gracenote – F

1) Play a C.
2) Play High A.
3) Play a C again.
4) Play an F.

C – High A, C Double Gracenote – High G

1) Play a C.
2) Play High A.
3) Play a C again.
4) Play High G.

C – High A, C Double Gracenote – High A

1) Play a C.
2) Play High A.
3) Play a C again.
4) Play High A.

D – High A, C Double Gracenote – D

1) Play a D.
2) Play High A.
3) Do a Strike to C finishing on a D.

D – High A, C Double Gracenote – E

1) Play a D.
2) Play High A.
3) Do a Strike to C finishing on an E.

D – High A, C Double Gracenote – F

1) Play a D.
2) Play High A.
3) Do a Strike to C finishing on an F.

D – High A, C Double Gracenote – High G

1) Play a D.
2) Play High A.
3) Do a Strike to C finishing on High G.

D – High A, C Double Gracenote – High A

1) Play a D.
2) Play High A.
3) Do a Strike to C finishing on High A.

E – High A, C Double Gracenote – D

1) Play an E.
2) Play High A.
3) Do a Strike to C finishing on a D.

E – High A, C Double Gracenote – E

1) Play an E.
2) Play High A.
3) Do a Strike to C finishing on an E.

E – High A, C Double Gracenote – F

1) Play an E.
2) Play High A.
3) Do a Strike to C finishing on an F.

E – High A, C Double Gracenote – High G

1) Play an E.
2) Play High A.
3) Do a Strike to C finishing on High G.

E – High A, C Double Gracenote – High A

1) Play an E.
2) Play High A.
3) Do a Strike to C finishing on High A.

F – High A, C Double Gracenote – D

1) Play an F.
2) Play High A.
3) Do a Strike to C finishing on a D.

F – High A, C Double Gracenote – E

1) Play an F.
2) Play High A.
3) Do a Strike to C finishing on an E.

F – High A, C Double Gracenote – F

1) Play an F.
2) Play High A.
3) Do a Strike to C finishing on an F.

F – High A, C Double Gracenote – High G

1) Play an F.
2) Play High A.
3) Do a Strike to C finishing on High G.

F – High A, C Double Gracenote – High A

1) Play an F.
2) Play High A.
3) Do a Strike to C finishing on High A.

High G – High A, C Double Gracenote – D

1) Play High G.
2) Play High A.
3) Do a Strike to C finishing on a D.

High G – High A, C Double Gracenote – E

1) Play High G.
2) Play High A.
3) Do a Strike to C finishing on an E.

High G – High A, C Double Gracenote – F
1) Play High G.
2) Play High A.
3) Do a Strike to C finishing on an F.

High G – High A, C Double Gracenote – High G
1) Play High G.
2) Play High A.
3) Do a Strike to C finishing on High G.

High G – High A, C Double Gracenote – High A
1) Play High G.
2) Play High A.
3) Do a Strike to C finishing on High A.

D – High A, D Double Gracenote – E
1) Play a D.
2) Play High A.
3) Play a D again.
4) Play an E.

D – High A, D Double Gracenote – F
1) Play a D.
2) Play High A.
3) Play a D again.
4) Play an F.

D – High A, D Double Gracenote – High G
1) Play a D.
2) Play High A.
3) Play a D again.
4) Play High G.

D – High A, D Double Gracenote – High A

1) Play a D.
2) Play High A.
3) Play a D again.
4) Play High A.

E – High A, D Double Gracenote – E

1) Play an E.
2) Play High A.
3) Do a Strike to D finishing on an E.

E – High A, D Double Gracenote – F

1) Play an E.
2) Play High A.
3) Do a Strike to D finishing on an F.

E – High A, D Double Gracenote – High G

1) Play an E.
2) Play High A.
3) Do a Strike to D finishing on High G.

E – High A, D Double Gracenote – High A

1) Play an E.
2) Play High A.
3) Do a Strike to D finishing on High A.

F – High A, D Double Gracenote – E

1) Play an F.
2) Play High A.
3) Do a Strike to D finishing on an E.

F – High A, D Double Gracenote – F

1) Play an F.
2) Play High A.
3) Do a Strike to D finishing on an F.

F – High A, D Double Gracenote – High G

1) Play an F.
2) Play High A.
3) Do a Strike to D finishing on High G.

F – High A, D Double Gracenote – High A

1) Play an F.
2) Play High A.
3) Do a Strike to D finishing on High A.

High G – High A, D Double Gracenote – E

1) Play High G.
2) Play High A.
3) Do a Strike to D finishing on an E.

High G – High A, D Double Gracenote – F

1) Play High G.
2) Play High A.
3) Do a Strike to D finishing on an F.

High G – High A, D Double Gracenote – High G

1) Play High G.
2) Play High A.
3) Do a Strike to D finishing on High G.

High G – High A, D Double Gracenote – High A
1) Play High G.
2) Play High A.
3) Do a Strike to D finishing on High A.

E – High A, E Double Gracenote – F
1) Play an E.
2) Play High A.
3) Play an E again.
4) Play an F.

E – High A, E Double Gracenote – High G
1) Play an E.
2) Play High A.
3) Play an E again.
4) Play High G.

E – High A, E Double Gracenote – High A
1) Play an E.
2) Play High A.
3) Play an E again.
4) Play High A.

F – High A, E Double Gracenote – F
1) Play an F.
2) Play High A.
3) Do a Strike to E finishing on an F.

F – High A, E Double Gracenote – High G
1) Play an F.
2) Play High A.
3) Do a Strike to E finishing on High G.

F – High A, E Double Gracenote – High A

1) Play an F.
2) Play High A.
3) Do a Strike to E finishing on High A.

High G – High A, E Double Gracenote – F

1) Play High G.
2) Play High A.
3) Do a Strike to E finishing on an F.

High G – High A, E Double Gracenote – High G

1) Play High G.
2) Play High A.
3) Do a Strike to E finishing on High G.

High G – High A, E Double Gracenote – High A

1) Play High G.
2) Play High A.
3) Do a Strike to E finishing on High A.

F – High A, F Double Gracenote – High G

1) Play an F.
2) Play High A.
3) Play an F again.
4) Play High G.

F – High A, F Double Gracenote – High A

1) Play an F.
2) Play High A.
3) Play an F again.
4) Play High A.

High G – High A, F Double Gracenote – High G
1) Play High G.
2) Play High A.
3) Do a Strike to F finishing on High G.

High G – High A, F Double Gracenote – High A
1) Play High G.
2) Play High A.
3) Do a Strike to F finishing on High A.

High G – High A, High G Double Gracenote – High A
1) Play High G.
2) Play High A.
3) Play High G again.
4) Play High A again.

The High A Double Gracenote is typically played between the first and last note of the embellishment.

Pictorial Index

This pictorial index will help identify an embellishment. The embellishments are sorted by the first note of the embellishment starting at Low G and then by the second note also starting at Low G.

Low G

Low G Gracenote / Strike to Low G	Birl / Low A Double Strike	Low A Triple Strike	B Grip / B Double Strike
B Triple Strike	B Taorluath	C Double Strike	C Triple Strike
Low G Half Doubling	Grip / D Double Strike	Heavy Throw	Taorluath
Bubly	D Triple Strike	D Throw / Throw on D	

Low A

Low A Gracenote / Strike to Low A	Low A Half Strike	A Birl / Half Double Strike	Half Triple Strike
Half Grip	Low A Half Doubling	E Double Strike	Half Pele / Half Hub-A-Dub
E Triple Strike			

B

B Gracenote	B Half Strike	Half Double Strike	Half Grip
Half Triple Strike	B Half Doubling	Half Pele / Half Hub-A-Dub	

C

C Gracenote / Strike to C	C Half Strike	Half Double Strike	Half Triple Strike
Half Grip	C Half Doubling	D Double Strike	D Triple Strike
Half Pele			

D

D Gracenote	D, Low G Double Gracenote / D Half Strike / D Grip	D Half Grip	Half Heavy Throw
Half Bubly	Half Double Strike / Half Grip	Half Triple Strike	Half Taorluath
D, Low A Double Gracenote	D, B Double Gracenote	D, C Double Gracenote / Half D Throw	Half Double Strike
Half Triple Strike	D Half Doubling	D Half Pele with Low G	D Half Pele with a C

E

E Gracenote	E, Low G Double Gracenote	Half Grip	E, Low A Double Gracenote / Half Strike
Half Double Strike	Half Triple Strike	E, B Double Gracenote	E, C Double Gracenote
E, D Double Gracenote	Half Doubling	F Double Strike	Half Pele
F Triple Strike			

F

F Gracenote	F, Low G Double Gracenote	Half Grip on a D	Half Grip
F, Low A Double Gracenote	F, B Double Gracenote	F, C Double Gracenote	F, D Double Gracenote
F, E Double Gracenote / Half Strike	Half Double Strike	Half Triple Strike	Half Doubling
High G Double Strike	Half Pele	High G Triple Strike	

High G

G Gracenote	High G, Low G Double Gracenote	Low G Doubling	Half Grip
High G, Low A Double Gracenote	G, Low A Strike	Low A Doubling	G Birl / G Double Strike
G Triple Strike	G Grip (Low A)	G Pele (Low A)	High G, B Double Gracenote
G, B Strike	B Doubling	G Double Strike	G Grip (B)
G Pele (B)	G Triple Strike	High G, C Double Gracenote	G, C Strike
C Doubling	G Double Strike	G Grip (C)	Tachum

G Pele (C)	G Triple Strike	High G, D Double Gracenote	G, D Strike
G, D Strike (C)	D Doubling	G Double Strike	G Grip (B)
G Grip (C) / G Double Strike (C)	G Pele (Low G)	G Pele (C)	G Triple Strike (Low G)
G Triple Strike (C)	High G, E Double Gracenote	G Strike	E Doubling
G Grip	G Double Strike	G Pele	G Triple Strike
High G, F Double Gracenote / G Doubling / G Half Strike	G Grip	F Doubling	G Strike

G Double Strike	Half Double Strike	G Pele	G Triple Strike
Half Triple Strike	High A Double Strike	Half Pele	High A Triple Strike

High A

High A Gracenote	High A, Low G, Double Gracenote	Low G Thumb Doubling	Half Grip
High A, Low A Double Gracenote	Thumb Strike (Low A)	Low A Thumb Doubling	Double Strike (Low) / Thumb Birl
Thumb Pele (Low A)	Thumb Grip	Thumb Triple Strike	High A, B Double Gracenote
Thumb Strike (B)	Thumb Doubling (B)	Thumb Double Strike (B)	Thumb Grip (B)
Thumb Pele (B)	Thumb Triple Strike (B)	High A, C Double Gracenote	Thumb Strike (C)
Thumb Doubling (C)	Thumb Double Strike (C)	Thumb Grip (C)	Thumb Pele (C)

Thumb Triple Strike (C)	High A, D Double Gracenote	Thumb Strike (D)	Thumb Strike (D) with a C
Thumb Doubling (D)	Thumb Grip (D) with a B	Thumb Grip (D) / Thumb Double Strike (Low G)	Thumb Double Grip (C)
Thumb Pele (D) with a Low G	Thumb Pele (D) with a C	Thumb Triple Strike (D) with a Low G	Thumb Triple Strike (D) with a C
High A, E Double Gracenote	Thumb Strike (E)	Thumb Doubling (E)	Thumb Grip (E)
Thumb Double Strike (E)	Thumb Pele (E)	Thumb Triple Strike (E)	High A, F Double Gracenote
Thumb Strike (F)	Thumb Doubling (F)	Thumb Grip (F)	Thumb Double Strike (F)

Thumb Pele (F)	Thumb Triple Strike (F)	High A, High G Double Gracenote	Thumb Strike (High G)
Half Double Strike (High G)	Thumb Grip (High G)	Thumb Double Strike (High G)	Thumb Pele (High G)
Half Triple Strike (High G)	Thumb Triple Strike (High G)		

www.ingramcontent.com/pod-product-compliance
Lightning Source LLC
Chambersburg PA
CBHW050848160426
43194CB00011B/2069